ADVANCE PRAISE

"I first met Heidi in fall of 2013. I was still reeling in grief following the murder of my six-year-old son, Dylan, at Sandy Hook Elementary School, and trying to figure out how I was going to create change in his name while supporting my surviving son, Jake. Heidi's organization, Camp Bow Wow, gifted us a therapy dog they had chosen and trained for Jake. Named 'Angel,' she not only provided peace and love for Jake, but she also helped fill some of the gaping hole Dylan's loss had left in our family. But personally, Heidi gave me more than just a wonderful dog.

"We shared our experience of loss—her husband, my son—the loss of focus and direction that followed, and then the overwhelming drive to do something positive as a result. Hearing about Heidi's experiences turning heartbreak into action reinforced my belief that I too could deliver transformational change. We became friends and fellow warriors. What I learned from Heidi is still relevant to me today: you never know when your life will launch.

"Though neither Heidi nor I chose the events that reshaped our lives and purpose, the following planning process, business thinking, problem-solving, motivation, persistence, and determination are the same. It is these lessons that are both shareable and learnable. SheFactor provides just that."

—NICOLE HOCKLEY, COFOUNDER AND MANAGING
DIRECTOR, SANDY HOOK PROMISE

"The most vivacious and talented woman I know. She has enormous energy and true grit. Through Heidi's ambition to help others, she has created an inspirational way to guide you down a path of empowerment. As a mother and politician with an extraordinary gift as an entrepreneur, she can guide young women to become resourceful when reaching for a higher level of self. I have watched and listened as Heidi's ideas and compassion lead you to think outside of the box to gain insight to meet your goals. SheFactor and Heidi Ganahl will give you the tools and resources you need to succeed."

—MARALEE MCLEAN, AUTHOR, NATIONAL
SPEAKER, CHILD ADVOCATE

"What a terrific way to mentor young women, grow our economy, and create a community of women who understand the vision to be economically, socially, and politically gifted. With the technology involved in this effort, SheFactor is an international movement to embrace girls and women around the world. Heidi has grabbed a star out of the sky for every newborn girl!"

—DR. TERRY NEESE, FOUNDER, INSTITUTE
FOR ECONOMIC EMPOWERMENT OF WOMEN;
PAST PRESIDENT, NATIONAL ASSOCIATION
OF WOMEN BUSINESS OWNERS

"As a twenty-three-year-old trying to pave my way in the world, it's been an incredible experience partnering with my mom to build a platform to launch my life, and in turn help others do the same. We hope it creates a community of dynamo ladies to inspire and empower each other to find their purpose and live a life they love!"

—TORI GANAHL, DAUGHTER OF HEIDI GANAHL

SHEFACTOR

Present Power – Future Fierce

HEIDI GANAHL

LIONCREST

PUBLISHING

SHEFACTOR

Present Power—Future Fierce

ISBN   978-1-5445-0186-4 *Hardcover*

      978-1-5445-1352-2 *Paperback*

      978-1-5445-1351-5 *Ebook*

      978-1-5445-0187-1 *Audiobook*

To all the beautiful young souls who are ready
to wander the path less traveled:

We've got your back.

CONTENTS

FOREWORD

Believe me, I've learned a lot of things the hard way. From my time on *The Bachelor* and *The Bachelorette* to starting my own businesses, I am no stranger to roses and the thorns that come in life. In my successes and failures, I've learned that the best flowers aren't the ones you win, but they're the ones you grow your own damn self (words I would've loved to tell twenty-five-year-old Kaitlyn).

Even though there's no way to cut corners and get out of life scot-free (believe me, I wish there were), this book would've been a great companion through every moment I've asked myself, *am I doing this right?* (or, more honestly, *what the f*** am I doing!?*)—the words cheering me on in the lows and the pat on the back during the highs (I mean, have you ever had a book give you a pat on the back? This book really is the whole package).

To give you some background, Heidi Ganahl didn't just

land a job right out of college—she landed THE job on the corporate ladder. When that fell short of her dreams, she started her own business...which just so happened to become a nationwide franchise. So yeah, she's got wisdom (and a lot of it).

With her impressive highlight reel, Heidi could stop there. But she doesn't. She shares the honest low points that accompany her successes and relates them to our own rollercoaster rides (let's be honest, we're all on one). She's lived head-over-heels love, survived sliding-down-the-wall heartbreak, and never questions whether any bit of it is off-limits. Heidi shares the inevitable twists and turns and shows that life is even more beautiful when it doesn't go exactly to plan.

SheFactor feels like a letter to any woman's younger self. It's sensitive, reassuring, and cuts the BS. Heidi empathizes with the confusing chatter that every woman faces (the paths that bosses, parents, friends, boyfriends, girlfriends think are best for us) and understands that every path is unique (and shouldn't be approached with a "cookie cutter"). In *SheFactor*, Heidi doesn't tell you what to do; she gives a microphone to your inner voice that already knows.

Kaitlyn Bristowe
Podcast Host, TV Personality, and Entrepreneur

INTRODUCTION

Ask questions. Surround yourself with inspiring people. Know you will fail. Learn to embrace failures as part of the process of evolution, growth and leveling-up. Get quiet regularly so you can listen to your gut—it always knows. Stay true to who you are and who you want to become!

—CARRIE DORR, FOUNDER AND CEO, LIFE SMART
X CARRIE DORR; FOUNDER, PURE BARRE

Congratulations! You're doing this "life" thing exactly as planned. You've taken all the right steps, and your path is stretching out in front of you as we speak. Whether you've got a college diploma, apprenticeship, or grand scheme in hand, you've done the legwork and are ready to start living. You'll soon have a couple job prospects waiting for you to choose from. You'll build your career for a few years, while investing in your friends and family, and remain open to the possibility of beautiful, fun relationships.

Eventually, one of those relationships will blossom into the engagement of your dreams and a storybook marriage. You'll both pursue your careers and enjoy a year or two of marriage, then the first baby will come. For a few weeks or months, you'll stay home with the baby, and when it's time to go back to work, you'll find exactly the right nanny or day care service who will love your little one while you return to pick up where you left off with your job until your second—maybe third, if you're adventurous—baby is born. Not too close together, not too far apart.

Life will go right back to normal as you juggle motherhood and your career for another couple of decades, and then you'll spend a carefree retirement catching up on things you've always wanted to do—using the money you've saved up throughout your successful and fulfilling career, of course.

Still with me?

That's the path that many of us set out on, anyway. I know I did, many years ago, and my daughter is where you are now. We all look to examples of prominent women who have "made it," and it looks like they have it all. Our families, teachers, and mentors move us along that path toward career and family, and we agree with them. It all looks like *such* a good plan.

The problem is, society's plan isn't really a plan at all. It's only an ideal. We usually don't figure out that the path we're on isn't working for us until life happens and things start to fall apart. We don't meet the right person at the right time, and our expected timelines become skewed. Or we're married with two kids, heading back into the workforce, realizing that "having it all" is not as easy as it's cracked up to be. Leaving kids at home becomes a more difficult decision than we could have known, or work starts to take us out of family events or moments in our kids' lives. Or the career we've fallen into isn't as fulfilling as we'd expected it to be, and we're stuck miserably counting down to five o'clock every single day.

It took my generation decades to realize there is more to life than that. My daughter's generation—you and your peers—seems to have a better handle on the need for balance. Your parents have raised you to have clear expectations of success and have set you on the right path to get there. You might have taken some time off after school to explore for a bit before you started your life, but the thing is, life is *still* going to start. In fact, some of you are already feeling that pressure—you've got student loans, a relationship, and bills and can't just take off to Europe to gather your bearings before it all hits. Life is happening now, and you've got to figure out how to cope—never mind how to thrive.

I've been there. I've had the path laid out in front of me,

ready for the taking. And I've had life implode around me, laughing in the face of my expectations. That moment—when you realize that society's ideals don't line up with reality—can be exhilarating or terrifying. For many in my generation, it didn't hit until we felt like it was too late to make a change. Many of us suddenly realized we were entrepreneurs at heart, and far too many pushed it off because they had two kids and a dog and no time to pursue their newfound goals.

That's why I'm so glad I can share these stories with you now. It's much better to figure out who you are and where *you* want to go sooner rather than later. That's not to say you can't get back on track, no matter where you are or where you wind up. I know because I've been there, and plenty of other women have been there as well. We all took wandering paths to where we ultimately needed to be, but the point is that we kept moving until we got there. I won't ever ask you to give up everything and start over. Instead, I want you to discover who it is you are and what kind of life you'll thrive in, and then I'm going to teach you how to hold yourself accountable to that path.

The SheFactor process, which we're going to walk through piece by piece in this book, is the framework that society's plans won't give you. It's how to figure out how you roll and what kind of work (and life!) will align best with that. The model of the superwoman who can do it all is a fantasy. Every woman around you who has found fulfillment in her life and career has only done so because they aligned their life with who they are at their core. They made it happen—not anyone else—and they did it in spite of what life threw at them.

My life oscillated between perfection and chaos for decades. I remember being twelve years old, riding in the back of our Pinto station wagon, crying as my grandparents, Orange County, and the life I knew faded away and the mountains of Colorado rolled past my window. In Colorado, I wound up with amazing experiences that would shape my future, including a full-ride scholarship to SMU—and then I promptly lost that same scholarship at the end of my freshman year. Just in time for my dad to lose his job and his ability to help me pay for school. I moved in with my grandparents in Southern California to attend a nearby college, worked two jobs, did an internship with an ad agency—and finally traversed my way back to CU Boulder to finish college a year later. I had the time of my life at CU (while still working a couple jobs and heading up public relations for Panhellenic), then promptly lost my boyfriend of three years, during senior year, when he married someone else without telling me first. (You really can't make this stuff up.)

The ups and downs didn't really stop. In fact, they became bigger and more painful. There were several earthquake moments in early adulthood that shook me to my core and threatened to take everything from me. The kind, bighearted, good-looking guy I married a couple years out of college was taken from me in a plane crash. The daughter I didn't plan for but loved and protected with all my heart was at risk for several years while I endured a long, expensive custody battle that exposed me to the corruption in the family court system. The multimillion-dollar business that I built from the dreams my late husband and I had was almost lost to the market crash of 2008.

Some of you will have earthquakes of your own. Others might only experience small tremors. No matter how your story unfolds, if you don't listen to your heart and your head, if you don't pay attention to what your gut or the universe is telling you to do, those moments will pull you completely off course. These are skills that take time and maturity to develop. But if you're willing to learn—from my ups and downs, from the other women who've shared in this book, and from the women willing to mentor you—I can help you get a jump on them.

If you were looking for another career book that would just tell you win big, this isn't it. But I hope you'll stick around, because I'm fed up with people acting like a job is all there is in life. That's not all that makes you happy. That's not what creates a life that you love. If a job is your biggest priority, why not build it out of something you love and are passionate about? The SheFactor steps we're going to walk through are meant to help you build a way of life, not just get a job. That's why careers are last on our list in this book. It's okay to take your time and work up to that.

I hope you're breathing a sigh of relief. When you're young and launching your life, that sudden pressure to be an immediate rock star in whatever you decide to do can be anxiety-inducing. You're just launching your life— how on earth are you supposed to know what you want to do with decades ahead of you?

Rather than setting the impossible expectation of knowing exactly what you're going to do and knocking it out of the park—you're going to play. You're going to be forgiving of yourself. You're going to listen to your intuition, do more of the things you love, and do less of the things you don't. You're crafting a whole life here. You should enjoy that process.

SHEFACTOR 101

SheFactor was born out of playfulness. Literally! When the pet care franchise that I started, Camp Bow Wow, grew to be the country's largest of its kind, we brought in a consultant to help us set goals from the corporate level down to an individual level. They did that by aligning everyone through a game. We took our corporate goals—increase sales by 20 percent, as an example—and broke them down into team goals. Each one of those goals moved the company forward. Each team had a role to play and goals to accomplish in order to be part of that bigger goal. Then we did the same thing for individuals—what do I have to do in order for my team to hit its goal, so the company can hit its goal? Every action that every person took had a purpose, and it was all framed inside of playfulness, with rewards, incentives, and cooperation driving us forward.

Then, I realized that we can do the same thing in our personal lives.

If you want to lose twenty pounds, you can't just *say* you want to lose twenty pounds. You need to identify the steps that will get you there. Maybe you need to work out, eat right, and stop drinking. Okay. But in order to accomplish those things, you'll need to do smaller things. To eat right, you might decide to make your lunch every day and cut back on carbs. Those steps came from having a vision for where you want to go, then figuring out how to tactically make that happen. So few of us make it down to the tactics. We set goals and have things we want, but we don't identify the tactics that will get us there or hold ourselves accountable to actually following through on those tactics. And we've found that accountability works best in that curious, playful spirit.

If you decide to make yourself lunch five times in a week, at the end of the week, check in on your score. Did you make it four out of five days? Awesome! That's 80 percent. Now how do you think you'll treat that fifth lunch next week? It's not just a lunch—it's the rest of your perfect score! You're going to be paying much closer attention so that your end-of-week score is higher.

The best part about this process is that it's *yours*. It's not me holding you to it. It's not your mom or your teacher or your boss. You're the only one responsible for your score. You can't make excuses to yourself, so it's more honest and authentic. (Okay, yes, I make excuses. A lot. I always try to do better, though!) But you also have the freedom to step back and reassess. You're in control. Why aren't you hitting those goals? Are the goals still in line with who you are and where you're going in life? Do the goals need to change or do your tactics need to change?

WHAT YOU CAN EXPECT IN THIS BOOK

There's so much we're going to cover in this book, and while I'm happy to share my story and my journey with you, I'm mostly excited to walk alongside you on your own journey. I want you to use the topics we cover as the pieces of the game that is the life you're building for yourself. It's not enough to look at successful women around you and hope that you'll get there one day. It's not enough to assume you know how they did it and model your life after them. You are the only you, and I want you to get to know yourself, find out what your goals really are, and start to enjoy the process of making those goals a reality. If you follow along and set this game up right, the prize at the end is a happy, successful life. It's looking back and saying, "Yes, that's exactly how I wanted to live my life this year. Now, where am I going next?"

The core of this concept is confidence. I want you to be confident in your potential and in the choices you make to reach it. You're going to achieve things at smaller levels and learn things along the way, and then you're going to roll those lessons and achievements into even bigger things down the road.

No one else can set those goals and expectations for you, so we're going to start by figuring out who you are and where you're going. Part I is all about your Present Power—who you are when all of the external noise fades away. We're going to look at who you are as a unique young woman, and we'll examine how knowing those personality strengths can help you along the way. We're going to look at what you love about life and how those passions can shape a life that you love. We're also going to identify the right group of people who will love and support you on this journey—your own personal SheFactor SEAL Team.

But no one else—not even your SEAL Team, which we'll talk about more throughout the book—can hold you accountable to your goals. Once you have a feel for the kind of life you want to build, you have to move the pieces of your life in that direction. If you aren't measuring those actions, there's no way to stay on track and accomplish what you're dreaming of. Like the games that got my company to reach our goals, Part II is going to break down the components of your Fierce Future into team and individual objectives. There are nine important things to measure: Folk, Flame, Faith, Freedom, Favor, Finance, Fashion, Fuel, and Future. For each of these Spheres, we'll talk about the tactical things you were probably expecting from a book like this—how to get the right job, have the right relationship, get healthy. But it might not be how you are used to getting it done.

This book is for the girl who wants to grow. You want to accomplish BIG things. You're not okay with the status quo. You don't just want to float along and let life happen to you. You're excited about your life and just need the right resources to unpack it, figure it out, and master it.

I'm here for you. You're going to identify a team to support you. I'll help you find a mentor, what I like to call a champion, to be there for you, and you're going to become that person you need for yourself as well. We're not here to pontificate or lay more expectations on your shoulders. We're here to get sh*t done. *Your* sh*t. Because you are your own SheFactor.

You've got this. Let's go.

PART I

PRESENT POWER: DISCOVERING WHO YOU ARE AND WHERE YOU'RE GOING

CHAPTER ONE

PERSONALITY

WHO YOU ARE AND HOW YOU ROLL

College graduation is an exciting time for all students. But with that excitement comes fears of proving yourself to the outside world, a challenge borne unequally by young women. The key is to believe in yourself and know that whatever you do with your life—and through all the twists and turns of your careers—you will make a positive impact on others.

Give yourself permission to change your mind about your hopes and dreams for a professional career. And know that your first post-college job will not be your last, so take some pressure off yourself in making that decision.

Above all, never forget to enjoy the ride. Know that the world awaits all of the great things you will accomplish!

—DR. DONNA SOCKELL, FOUNDER, CENTER FOR EDUCATION ON SOCIAL RESPONSIBILITY, LEEDS SCHOOL OF BUSINESS, UNIVERSITY OF COLORADO, BOULDER; AND PRESIDENT, SB EDUCATIONAL CONSULTANTS

I was raised to be very driven. There were some competing messages about the execution of my life—Mom wanted me to get an eight-to-five and settle down, Dad wanted me to get out and try whatever I could—but the basic expectation was that I would go out into the world and kick some butt. I was surrounded by incredible women who inspired and encouraged me to live life in a big way. I didn't want to get a job—I wanted to run the corporation. I didn't want to just play soccer—I wanted to be an Olympic medalist. I ran for student council and played soccer, was on the pom-pom team and prom court, and did everything I could to make my mark in the world.

The women in my life—aunts, grandmothers, mom—didn't take no for an answer. From my mother who stayed at home when I was young, to my aunt who was an advertising exec, to my other aunts, close friends of my mom whom I called "aunt," and my grandmothers, they all modeled to me that you do what you want in life without taking any BS. That you deserve no less than the absolute best that the world has to offer.

As a result, when people ask me what it was like being a *woman* in a startup or a *woman* in business or a *woman* as the CEO of a $100 million company, I have to laugh. It honestly never occurred to me that being a woman made me different or posed a challenge. It wasn't until I was selling my company, years down the road, that I realized I was the only woman in the room once the investment bankers rolled in.

But being a "woman in business" was never my story.

My story is that I was always scrappy. I was born to young parents—eighteen and twenty when I entered the world—who worked hard to get by. My dad was working three jobs around then, and he later became a cop. My mom stayed home with us until later in life, when she worked her way up to a leadership position in our town. They taught me to never take my opportunities for granted. I was driven and ready to change the world right out of high school. But when I made it out of Colorado and into college in Texas, it wasn't quite the world I was expecting.

THE GOLDEN HANDCUFFS

Southern Methodist University is a small private school in Dallas, where I saw my first Louis Vuitton bags and Rolex watches. It didn't take long to figure out that the school wasn't *me*. I didn't fit in very well at first, and by the time

I figured out how to settle in, I had lost my scholarship (focused more on the social scene than studying). Because it was one of the most expensive schools in the country, that was a deal breaker for my parents. Plan B was Pepperdine University, which was holding a half-ride scholarship for me, until my dad lost his job over that first summer.

Plan C to the rescue: move in with my grandparents and work full time while attending Cal State Fullerton. For a year, I worked nonstop, until my dad got back on his feet and I decided to finish up at the University of Colorado at Boulder.

See? Scrappy. Always plowing forward, always adapting.

After graduation, I missed Southern California and my grandparents, so I went back out to live with them and land my dream job. (Of course I'd expect to get my dream job right out of college.) And I did, actually, at least for a while. I singled out an ad agency—my dream since childhood, in the footsteps of my aunt and uncle—started out as a receptionist, then worked my way up to an account manager. Although I had plenty of adventures in San Diego (more on those later in the book) and loved the work I was doing, I wasn't making enough to live on my own. I moved back home, Denver this time, and found that Colorado didn't have quite the robust advertising market of Southern California.

As much as I loved the creativity and freedom inside ad agencies, I struggled to find a job. Outside of being a cop, my dad had worked in sales his whole life, and he suggested I give it a try. "It's a good job," he said, and he pointed me toward an opening in pharmaceutical sales.

He wasn't wrong, really. It was a good job, and I didn't have to worry about my budget anymore. But oh my goodness, it was boring. Deliver samples, convince doctors to prescribe the drugs on the formulary, then do it all again. Then there was the catering—feeding the office staff was the ticket in to see the doctor, and we didn't have DoorDash back then.

This is the stage in my life that I refer to as "the golden handcuffs."

It was hard to complain. The benefits were great and so was the pay. But I was missing something. There was a void. For as driven as I've always been, I also have a deep need for creativity, risk-taking, and entrepreneurial-based freedom. This job offered nothing like that.

Yet there I stayed, for eight long years. I was in pharmaceutical sales when I met Bion, my first husband. I was in pharmaceutical sales when he and I started dreaming about something bigger and sketched out Camp Bow Wow's business plan on a bar napkin. I was in pharmaceutical sales when I lost him to a plane crash and my life was turned upside down.

It started on a beautiful Colorado day in May of '94.

First thing that morning, my husband, Bion, jumped from bed, gave me a quick kiss and a "love ya babe," and headed out to meet my folks for his twenty-fifth birthday surprise.

A couple weeks prior, my dad had run into an old family friend from Monument—Cliff, who was a United Airlines pilot of thirty years. My dad came home excited about Cliff's new hobby doing air shows in a vintage stunt plane.

It was the perfect surprise birthday gift for my young daredevil husband.

The plane had done all the stunts. Cliff had radioed to my parents that he was going to do a flyby over them, so they could take pictures before he landed. Instead, the plane crashed, and Bion and Cliff were killed instantly.

I was devastated.

As I lay in bed for days—weeks, so sad and lost—my dogs, Mick and Winnie, would nudge me with their wet noses or give me a quick "WOOF" to remind me we still needed to go out and play ball, and to remind me that life hadn't stopped.

Because of the way that formularies were affected by shifts in healthcare legislation, we were always getting hired and laid off and hired again. I had just been laid off before the crash, and I could have gotten a job again as soon as I wanted it. But my life was in a tailspin, and with a $1 million settlement check in hand, I needed a change. The golden handcuffs were broken, and I needed to get away while I could.

SOMETHING MORE IN STORE

There's so much more I'll get to share with you about that phase of my life—how I lost more than just $1 million, how I learned about myself and others, and how I gained a life I couldn't have imagined. But the most important detail for now is that I decided to get out of those cuffs for good.

After a quick, rocky, rebound marriage to an old friend, then a long, even worse divorce, I made a last-ditch effort to support myself and my young daughter. My brother literally took me to the bank to pull out the last $80,000 of the settlement and pulled out those napkin-sketched plans to give Camp Bow Wow a try. I was back in pharmaceutical sales to pay the bills, but my little brother and I worked Camp Bow Wow on the side. He ran the day-to-day operations, while I took the helm for marketing, the books, and everything on the backend. Tori, then five years old, and I would walk to the busiest parks near our location every afternoon to hand out Milk-Bones with flyers for a free first visit. By the time we'd built it up enough to start a second location, I was able to quit pharmaceutical sales for good.

I was free, and the difference was night and day.

Every day, I worked my tail off for Camp Bow Wow (pun intended), and every morning I was excited to jump out of bed and do it all again. I loved every minute of it. It was more than a job—in pharmaceutical sales, I wasn't all in. Half the time, I'd blow off my work. I'd go golfing and hang out with friends. Even though I'd been driven for my entire life, that job took it all out of me. It was terrible.

What I wish I had known back then is that it wasn't just the job that made the difference. It'd be easy to think that being an entrepreneur was energizing and having "a job" was draining, but that wasn't it. My internship at the ad agency in California was just as invigorating, while some entrepreneurial efforts before Camp Bow Wow were a drag. And there did come a point at Camp Bow Wow when it became a job again—the more *corporate* and *in the weeds* the work became, the less I enjoyed it.

It was the creativity that I loved. I was drawn to building brands, doing marketing, running PR, figuring out messaging, and creating something that people could fall in love with. That was my *thing*. It was something deep within me, which I now know was my Silhouette—a framework to understand how you operate and that has taught me so much about myself and others.

DREAMERS, STORYTELLERS, CONQUERORS, AND MORE

A good friend of mine introduced me to the concept of personality archetypes, and it changed my perspective completely. A lot of people resist this sort of framework because they don't want to be put into a box. It's not about that, though. Identifying my Silhouette (I'm a Dreamer!) explained so much for me—*oh my Gosh, that's why I do this thing! And that's why I do that other thing!* I realized why I'd always driven my mother and brother a bit nuts, why I was always the idea store, why I hated boring meetings and couldn't stand going over scores of data in one sitting.

Identifying my personality traits, strengths, and weaknesses didn't mean I would only live that exact type of life from there on out. What it really gave me was permission to be myself. I understood more about who I was, and as I learned how to identify other people's Silhouettes, I could understand more about them as well. My right-hand gal at the time was a Guardian, so I realized she was always going to make sure that people knew she cared. My mom is a Conqueror, so she's always going to be the taskmaster who gets sh*t done. Today, I know my husband is a Director who doesn't want to be boxed in. No wonder he does the opposite whenever I ask him to do something a certain way—ha!

Knowing more about my Silhouette and the people around me, I can approach situations with better perspective. I can set up my teams in a different way. I can walk into projects that are outside of my strengths in a different way. If I'm going into a data-intensive project, I can pick an Explorer to work with me on it. If I need some big-vision effort, I'll find another Dreamer, and we'll tackle it together.

This framework is magical. And at this stage in your life, it can make your decisions so much easier. If you know you're a Dreamer like me, you probably won't want to pursue a career around data entry. For this chapter and the next, we'll spend a lot of time looking back on our lives to see what really drives us at our core. From childhood, I showed signs of being a Dreamer. I was always going to do something big and free and exciting. We'll also look for some role models that we can identify with— not just based on their external success, but their internal motivation. When you identify other women who share

THE SEVEN SILHOUETTES

Here are the personality Silhouettes we've created to help you figure out how you're wired, what makes you tick, and how you relate to those around you. The SheFactor Silhouettes are based on a blend of various tools and archetype systems out there. This approach changed my perspective of myself and the people around me. You might be able to tell which one you align with just by these descriptions. Or, you can download the SheFactor app and take the quiz!

- Director: Spontaneous, innovative, and artistic. A bit rebellious, and always ready for an adventure, don't box them in. Directors are typically musicians, innovators, actors, entrepreneurs, trendsetters, and artists. They love their projects and LOVE to create—businesses, environments, buildings, paintings, and ideas. Day-to-day life can be a bit of a bore and can drive them to jump from one grand idea to the next. Don't expect them to follow a schedule or routine, and expect some swings from brooding and serious to the life of the party. They follow the latest fashion trends and do not thrive in cubicles. They want to be appreciated for their work. Directors and their creative drive can leave a trail of unfinished projects at work, but oh what fantastic creativity and innovation is harnessed when they get the job done! Famous Director women include Princess Di, Lady Gaga, Scarlett Johansson, Anne Hathaway, and Ashley Judd.

- Storyteller: Lighthearted, fun to be around, great communicator. Storytellers are natural performers; they love applause and sharing their love of life with as many people as they can. Their spoken words are everything. They're usually entertainers, teachers, and leaders. They are expressive, charming, intuitive, dynamic, and rarely boring. They can tap into their inner wisdom in a heartbeat. They enjoy playing to the audience and can be very persuasive to an individual or a big audience. They can also be "drama queens" and a bit demanding when it comes to the attention of those around them, but they are just plain fun. Storytellers often give voice to what's happening in our culture. They are typically polished, classy, and graceful. Famous Storyteller women include Tina Fey, Mindy Kaling, Angelina Jolie, and Amy Poehler.

- Guardian: Healer, caretaker, devoted to others. Guardians are typically doctors, nannies, teachers, or in the service industry. They are inspiring beings who deserve praise and gratitude for the good they do in the world. They typically live a somewhat simple life and are not as driven to make lots of money. They like to control the situation, especially if they are in charge of how others' needs are met. Guardians don't mind routine tasks, and they like to work behind the scenes. They'll work long hours with a smile on their face and are not flashy in their dress or look. It's important to praise the Guardians in our life as they need to be appreciated and told their work is worthy. They typically present themselves as sweet, trustworthy, and friendly—they're the friend we go to for comfort and care. Famous Guardian women include Kristen Stewart, Mother Teresa, and Queen Elizabeth II.

- Dreamer: Inspirational, uplifting, and a motivator. The Dreamer challenges people to be the best they can be. They think BIG! Big ideas, big approaches, and big expectations of those around them. They're coaches, counselors, and business leaders. Dreamers are always on a mission—late to bed and early to rise. They rarely let a day go by without finding a way to improve themselves or the people around them. Compassionate, with a natural ability to connect with people, Dreamers are warm and nurturing to be around. They are at home in front of a crowd but can get a bit arrogant sometimes with all the attention they get and their claim to the moral high ground. The good news is they usually follow their own advice and get credit for their drive to improve the world. Famous Dreamer women include Kate Middleton, Amy Adams, and Oprah.

- Conqueror: Strategist, defender, and a doer. The Conqueror likes to create and enforce challenges, rules, and plans. They're usually physicians, athletes, lawyers, and strategists. They are determined, very organized, and love a challenge. Conquerors are fearless soldiers who will go right to the front line in any battle yet harbor a nurturing soft side that's protective of their loved ones. They may not be eloquent communicators, but they sure do have the street smarts that others lack. Conquerors love physical activity, and when they play, they play hard. They can be emotional and a bit hot-tempered, but they are always there for those around them. They have a ton of energy! Famous Conqueror women include Hillary Clinton, Ronda Rousey, and Lea Michele.

- Queen: Born leader, commanding presence, and driven. The Queen is a leader no matter what her role is. She's usually an organizer like a president, general, or CEO, though she can execute as much leadership as an admin assistant or anywhere she finds herself. Queens see the big picture, know how to delegate, and can quickly assess a situation and lead people to action. They expect loyalty and are demanding on those around them. They are skilled at solving tough problems and stick with it until the job is done. Queens are charismatic, and their take-charge energy is almost palpable. There are not many Queens out there, so if that's your Silhouette, own it sister! Famous Queens include Beyoncé, Khloe Kardashian, and Martha Stewart.

- Explorer: Teachers, information gatherers, and philosophers. Explorers love knowledge above all and like to experiment. They're usually students, tech geeks, adventurers, authors, and researchers. Explorers absorb knowledge and share it with others, often found surrounded by books, podcasts, and TED talks—though they aren't fond of public affection or conflict. They are curious, intellectual, and very logical. Explorers are also pretty easy-going and more reserved than the other Silhouettes. They don't really like conflict, but they are reliable and willing to bravely try things others won't, especially when the data shows it's the right thing to do. And Explorers are willing to compromise. They are typically an authority on some subject and surround themselves with people who share the love of information. Famous Explorer women include Gloria Steinem, Michelle Obama, and Sandra Bullock.

your Silhouette, you understand more about why they do what they do and how they got to where they are.

TAKING OFF THE MASK

Back when I had those golden handcuffs, I wasn't bad at playing the Storyteller game. I did what I needed to in order to pay the bills and support my little family. But I was still a Dreamer. Faking it is called "masking," and people do it all the time. We pretend that we know, care, and are interested when deep down we know we're not being real. A lot of us are really good at it. But at the end of the day, it's still inauthentic. Eventually, people are going to see through you, or like me, you'll be left with a void.

On the other hand, when I can step into my role as a Dreamer and give a motivational speech, or inspire my management team, or lead a big initiative, people will get it. They'll be completely into it and ready to take action. And a chief financial officer could stand up to talk about numbers and be just as inspiring.

In the world of social media and filtered, curated lives, we're used to masking. We create personas that will draw people to us. We worry about how we're seen by the outside world much more than whether we're being authentic and aligning with who we really are. One thing I learned in marketing, though, was that your image could be amazing in every aspect, but if it failed in authenticity, the campaign would fail as well. If you try to market Coca-Cola as a healthy drink or Snickers as an energy bar, deep down inside we all know it's junk.[1] Those messages will never hold. When you live a life that doesn't match who you are, it's never going to feel right—even if you have all the markers of external success.

Being authentic is going to mean saying no to things that seem to make sense on the surface, but intuitively we know are missing the mark. I think of Blue Apron, the food delivery service who hit that niche of us who don't have time to go to the grocery store and prepare healthy foods. But they knew that their niche had to be the people who could afford their service in order to check off that box of having a few healthy meals a week. They didn't pretend to be the answer for the family of five living on a budget. They know what they are and don't try to be anything else. We also see Apple, Nike, and lululemon in this category. They've got niches nailed.

---

1   Truth in Advertising. "Do Snickers Really Satisfy?" Retrieved on 12/28/2018: https://www.truthinadvertising.org/snickers-really-satisfy/

Successful companies have a strong vision and identity around their brand. That's how we found so much success with Camp Bow Wow. So many people wanted us to open dog retail clothing stores or add in doggy spa services, but that wasn't what we were about. We just wanted to create a happy, healthy environment for dogs to be themselves so that owners wouldn't feel guilty when they were away. That's it. I wouldn't let anyone drag us off of that vision. That's what we have to do with our lives as well.

WHO YOU ARE DETERMINES WHERE YOU'RE GOING

We're starting with personality, before any other future-based actions, because "success" isn't a one-stop shop. There is no benchmark for net worth or career success or lifetime achievements that can serve as a happy life. The success that Oprah has found has come very differently than that of Tina Fey, even though they are both in similar fields with similar achievements. In the field you pursue, you'll find different women have made it work for them in different ways. It's important to identify with someone who shares your Silhouette, so that when you model after her, are mentored by her, or are inspired by her, it's in ways that will be authentic in your own life.

If you aren't yet sure what your Silhouette is, take a minute to think about the way that you dream about your life. What motivates you? When I implemented games at

Camp Bow Wow to motivate my team, everyone could choose their own incentive. They could choose between comp time, flex time to work from home, and monetary bonuses or increases in base pay. For one year, they could choose to go for bonuses to save for a house down payment, for example, and the next year, they could choose flex time to enjoy that new home. Surprisingly, those categories were perfectly split across the board. Not everyone chose the money; some wanted the freedom to take an extra day off to ski. It created a much happier workforce.

Those incentives and dreams will align not only with your circumstances but with who you are as a person. A lot of people think that Dreamers and entrepreneurs are motivated by money, when in reality we're driven by freedom. Most of us don't do what we do for the paycheck; we often don't even realize we've "made it" in terms of financial success. We're in it for the achievement and the freedom.

A Storyteller will be incentivized by praise for the words they say, while a Dreamer wants praise for being inspirational. Then there's the Explorer, who wants acknowledgment for their analysis, and the Conqueror who wants praise for getting sh*t done. Guardians want to know they cared for you well, and Directors want lavish acknowledgment for their creativity and ingenuity. And then there are the Queens, who just want it all.

The more you understand about yourself, what motivates you, and what inspires you, the more you can break free of external expectations and be able to dream of the life you want to build for yourself. It's okay to rebel against the structures that you or other people have placed in your life. That's not to say that you're going to identify this persona, then shed your job and degree and life and run away into something else. It takes time to shape the life you really want to live, and there's no reason to rush into it. This is a process. It's a mindset, and it's a game.

We're not here to go all or nothing. That's why we're not starting with career. We're painting on the canvas of your life, and that means stretching beyond the limits that life tends to place on us when we're young. This is a process of discovery—who are you really, when you strip away the masks and expectations? What can that uncover about what you enjoy, hate, and need more of?

Wouldn't it be cool if you and your boyfriend understood each other's Silhouettes and could laugh at the fights you've been having instead of things blowing up? Wouldn't it be cool if you could understand your parents, your friends, or your boss more? Wouldn't it be cool to understand yourself more?

If someone gave you this book, it's because they didn't figure this stuff out for themselves for a very long time.

It's because they were able to give you every other tool to succeed—but they didn't know how to articulate this one. The one that helps you uncover who you are, where you're going, and how you can get yourself there.

You've got to be brave for this. It's not an easy thing to dig this deep and push yourself this hard. I don't want to diminish this step; you won't just take a test, figure yourself out, then change your life. It's hard work to stay aligned with who you are deep down, but the rewards are so great. If you can get to that place of being in your authentic self and understanding how you roll, you'll also find confidence in your decisions and in knowing that you've got this. You'll know how to be nimble and adjust your life when things don't go as planned. You'll know how to spot signs and honor the universe and your intuition when it tells you to shift. And in the rest of the book, you'll gain the tools and practice to make that shift and get things done.

It starts here. There's no way to get this from anyone else. It has to be internal. If you want an amazing life, you have to know who's living it. It has to be authentic, or it'll never be fulfilling—and that's what we're all looking for anyway.

PAUSE AND PRACTICE

Stop! Before you keep reading, it's time to put this stuff into action. Take some time to identify your Silhouette. If you already have the SheFactor app, you can take the quiz to find out. Take some time to see how that Silhouette has played out in your life and how it might shape your future. For a bonus exercise, pick a few key people in your life and try to identify their Silhouette. It'll help you interact with them in a much more effective way. Join the conversation about personality, authenticity, and our true selves with the hashtag #myshefactor.

CHAPTER TWO

PASSION

WHAT MAKES YOU JUMP OUT OF BED IN THE MORNING?

Compare leads to despair! No one tells you when you graduate it's perfectly normal not to know exactly what you want to do. So when it feels like everyone around you has it all together, resist the temptation to compare yourself to others. Some actually may, but many don't. And it's all okay!

—RENÉE ISRAEL, COFOUNDER OF DOC POPCORN, AS WELL AS HER LATEST VENTURE, WISDOMWRKS

The difference between life in the golden handcuffs and later on running a business my way was incredible. I found my spark again. I was able to be creative, think about the big picture, and make things happen. While it took me a long time to get there, I've never regretted shaking off that glamorous pharmaceutical job and stepping out into the unknown to create Camp Bow Wow.

When the business started to take off, consultants told me to hire C-level executives to help me—CLO, CFO, etc.—who were my opposites. Because of that, they didn't understand my leadership style and we would butt heads. I came to realize that if you want someone to share your vision, they need to share a little flavor of who you are. This is something that I learned through a group called Vistage I was involved with, which is a networking and coaching group for CEOs.

I was struggling to gain my footing with the company growing so quickly, and I knew I had to figure out how to best lead us forward. Don, my Vistage coach, noticed this and told me, "I think I have someone you should meet. She might be able to help you find your grounding as a leader."

The first thing she helped me do was identify my Silhouette, like we just did in the previous chapter. The assessment showed me clearly that I was a Dreamer, and over the next several times that we met, we talked about my leadership style. We talked about what I was good at and what I enjoyed doing at the company. We talked about the people I was surrounding myself with.

She pointed out that the people I'd been hiring were very different than me, and *then* she did something that changed me:

She gave me permission.

She gave me the okay to hire someone who was a Dreamer just like me, or similar—like a Guardian or Director—so that they would honor my Silhouette as a leader without trying to replace me. Underneath this permission to hire a Heidi-style leader came another layer: the permission to be myself.

I grew up passionate about doing big things. I was visionary. I didn't like diving into the details of the work I was doing as much as driving long-term plans—instead, I'd always make projects bigger than they needed to be. Ask little Heidi if she wanted to build a lemonade stand, and instead I'd want to turn it into a lemonade *company* with national distribution and cohesive branding!

Even if I didn't think it was *wrong* for me to be that way, I at least knew I was a little bit different than the other kids.

She gave me permission to not only be myself in that way, but to be excited, happy, and unapologetic about it. We see this kind of ownership show up when someone gets diagnosed with dyslexia or a personality disorder later in life, then they suddenly blossom. When they get, understand, and accept themselves, they often begin to thrive.

Identifying my Silhouette and becoming comfortable with who I was as a person changed my perspective entirely. Instead of beating myself up over the things I didn't enjoy or excel at, I accepted that not everything could be my strength. I could start to live for the things that make me jump out of bed in the morning, and I let go of the need to be good at everything else.

This isn't easy at first. When you're young, there's some *fake it til you make it* involved in starting a career. Or, when you're an entrepreneur and running a startup, you have to do everything yourself for a while. If you don't have the money to hire people, you have to just wing it for some tasks, even if you aren't good at them. And there will be things you're not good at. I earned a master's in healthcare administration, but it didn't teach me about depreciated equity or why the books are done in a certain way. Even now, as a regent in charge of a $5 billion organization, financials are still not my favorite part of the job. Don't get me wrong, I've learned to be good at analyzing and understanding them, but it's not something I enjoy much. The same goes for legal documents; people send me eighteen-page documents that lose my interest by the sixth page.

While I'd been trying to excel at everything—to be good

at HR, good at finance, good at operations, and to hire someone who fit all of those boxes too—really, it was branding, strategy, and vision that I was actually *good* at. Those are the things that lit a fire inside of me. I only had to know enough to be dangerous in the other fields, or just enough to get by until someone else could take them over. Why? Because HR, finance, and operations are someone else's passion.

Later on, when Camp Bow Wow grew even more, I taught my franchisees to do the same thing. I'd help them figure out what they were really good at and where they weren't so great, then encourage them to not force themselves into their weak spots. In other words, you don't have to do something just because you think it's something a leader *should* do. The best leaders find the right person for each role so that they can each focus on the things that they're great at.

A NIGHT-AND-DAY DIFFERENCE

The more you embrace your Silhouette, the easier it is to uncover your passion and create a life that's in line with it. Or, in a more practical sense, focusing on your passion is about figuring out what you're good at, what your talents are, then letting go of the expectation that you have to be good at everything else as well.

When you get this right, the work becomes so much more

fun. Once you know how you roll, how you interact with others, and what makes you tick, you can see that we all have a space to fill. If you're the triangle, you don't need to try to fit into the circle space anymore. If you're really good at sales and know that you're going to flourish in building relationships with people, then *excel* at that and let yourself only have a passing competence in Excel.

Taking that worry off of your plate is incredibly freeing.

Another way to learn about yourself is by creating a Mind Map. Mind Mapping is a very creative and logical way of note-taking that visually "maps out" your ideas.

All Mind Maps have a structure that starts from the center and uses lines, symbols, words, colors, and images to convert a long list of your thoughts into a colorful, organized diagram that works in line with your brain's natural way of doing things.

One way to understand a Mind Map is by thinking of it like a tree. There are the root ideas, the branches that extend from the trunk, and the leaves that come from the branches.

You can put your ideas down in any order—start with a circle in the middle and begin to branch out from there. Free-form it and don't worry too much about structure;

worry about reorganizing them later. You can see an example on the next page of what it might look like to map out getting a job in an industry you love; the example used is nature.

If we could get a window into pre-Camp Bow Wow Heidi to see my Mind Map, we might see things like animals, creativity, building things, and helping other people all connected on the page. Building a business around having a doggy day care, hanging out with dogs, creating the marketing material, and helping other people open their franchises fell right in the middle of things that sparked passion in me.

And I wasn't managing the units either. Once they were built out, the franchisees ran them. I was free to be creative and to do the high-level processes; I believe that's why it became so successful.

When I was in pharmaceutical sales, I had a "great job." Life was happening just as it was supposed to, and it had all the external markers of success. But I was *bored*.

Because it was such a great job, I didn't feel like I could quit. I would have been lectured by everyone around me. At the same time, because I was so restless, I wasn't performing well. In everything else in life, I'd been a superstar. But I couldn't make it happen.

When I started Camp Bow Wow, those same people around me told me I was being ridiculous. It was a waste of money; it didn't make sense; I shouldn't do it. At some point, I realized that I'd tried everything that they'd told me was sensible—every external expectation—and nothing had worked. The reason these things didn't work is because they weren't things I was passionate about. Allergy and asthma equipment distributor, baby-bedding catalog retailer, and a financial advisor. Nope.

What would my life have held if I started out from a place of passion?

What will your life look like if you do?

Society doesn't necessarily want you to answer that question, because it raises the bar for everyone. If you're successful by following your passion instead of the path already laid out for you by others, then they'll be expected to do that same brave work. I want more for you than that. There are people in your life who love you who want more for you. *You* want more for you. Let yourself dream, raise the bar, and do the work that will change your life.

IDENTIFY YOUR PASSION

Asking yourself to identify your passion is a pretty broad question. For instance, you might be completely on board with this concept but not sure exactly what your passion is. To overcome this challenge, I like to have people do an inventory of what they love to do. Make a list. Whether it's in your current job or life or in the future, what do you enjoy? What does a perfect day look like? What would a perfect job be? Would you rather be on the phone all day, behind a computer, or out doing sales calls? Carry a small notepad with you or create a note on your phone and just log this for a few days.

Then, start to take a more holistic view of your answers to those questions. Start to see some themes. Is it creativity that you really love, or data and numbers? Do you love people and building relationships? Look for common threads or themes in the things that you absolutely love, as well as in the things you don't like to do. Connect this with your Silhouette and what it says about you.

This doesn't have to be a complicated exercise either. A yellow pad of paper can be plenty to help you figure out a whole lot about yourself. Write down activities you absolutely hate in your job or your life, as well as the things you love, because they can both give you insight. If you hate working out but you want to get fit, maybe seeing that you love to spend time with people can help. Maybe you could get a friend to walk around the park with you.

Another way to identify passion points in your life is to look at the people you've wanted to model your life after. Do you want your life to be like Kate Hudson the actress, Peggy Whitson the astronaut, or Kayla Itsines the workout queen? Look at the coworkers, friends, and mentors you've looked up to as well. What specifically are these people doing that you admire?

The most important thing to remember at this point is that you can be playful about this. I'm not asking you a serious question that requires a serious answer. Let your mind wander around your dreams for the future, things you love to do, and how you'd like your life to look. We're not going to worry about reality for a while. Let it go, because that's the only way you're going to let loose and dream. It's the only way you'll free yourself of your pre-determined notions of what your life should be.

SHAKE OFF THE SHOULDS

I recently read a book called *Designing Your Life*, and in it there was the story of a man that felt so familiar. In some ways, I've lived it, my peers have lived it, and all too often, I see the girls I work with living it too. It was about a guy whose mom wanted him to be a civil engineer. That's what his dad did, and his dad before that. So that's what he did. He went to Stanford, got his degree in civil engineering...and he hated it. Every single day, this brilliant kid hated his job.

But he had something special: his company worked with him. Someone close to him said, "I want you to keep a diary throughout your day. I want you to write down when you're feeling energized, when you feel low, when you like things, and when you don't. Keep track of everything, and then let's talk."

Through this exercise, they figured out that he didn't like writing reports at all. He loved figuring out how to solve problems and strategizing at a high level, but when he had to draw it all up into reports, he lost all of that energy. He was really in his element when he was thinking creatively. When he took that information to his bosses, they worked out a solution. By giving him an assistant, his time was freed to focus on the part of being a civil engineer that tapped into his creativity, problem-solving, and strategic, high-level thinking. In this way, he was able to enjoy his job and the life he'd chosen.

There's so much I love about this story, not the least of which is the way that this guy identified his strengths and pursued a life that he could love. What's truly special about it, though, is the way that he worked within his existing framework and that the people around him were there to support him. He didn't throw up his hands and quit his job. He didn't take off to Europe to find himself. He dug deep for some self-awareness and identified ways to honor his strengths within his circumstances.

While the things we're working on in this book are building toward your future, it's important to not force that future. It's too easy to decide we *should* be good at this or *should* enjoy that, but it doesn't tell us anything about who we are or what we're great at and passionate about. At the same time, it's not practical to think we can identify a far-off future and jump right into it today. From my story so far, would you guess that my future would wind up in education or in politics? I know I didn't.

Identifying your passion and giving yourself permission to pursue it is about your instincts, not your expectations. So we're going to look back, not forward, to discover them.

MAP IT OUT

You can't know what you'll be doing ten or fifteen years down the road, but the essence of who you *are* won't change much over time. The things that I loved to do in high school and college are the same things I love to do now—being creative, problem-solving, working in team environments, building new things. I didn't know at the time that these were core parts of me. I didn't see them as passion points. If you can identify what you're passionate about now, you might save ten years of struggling trying to figure it out.

The exercise I find most helpful here is Mind Mapping. Let's take another hypothetical scenario as an example and walk through the exercise together. Let's say you're set to graduate within the next year—maybe less than a year! But you've discovered a problem. Your degree path is set, and as you dig into who you are and what your passions have always been, you find that what you've chosen is really not for you. It feels like a massive mistake.

Before you panic, you decide to get your thoughts in order. The important thing about Mind Mapping is to not attach any emotion to it. You don't have to judge it or complain about it or even feel whiny about complaints. It's just a list, just information. You pull out some paper, take some deep breaths, and start making a list.

A Mind Map starts simple: with everything that comes to mind.

When you think about what you enjoy now, what you enjoyed as a kid, what has always given you energy and life—what comes up? Write down your hobbies, your pursuits in high school, what you do to decompress, where you love to be, accomplishments that made you feel especially proud, jobs you've loved, tasks you've loved—everything that gives you joy and fulfillment in your life.

The more you write, the more patterns you'll likely see. Circle things that are similar and connect them with simple lines. At first, maybe nothing will seem to go together. Or if it does, the connections you make might not feel realistic. That's okay. Keep mapping.

The great thing about Mind Mapping is that you can just keep going and going until you find your answers. When you look at a big, sprawling tree, the tiniest branches on one side of a tree seem so far away from the other side—but eventually, they all connect. Like the branches moving into the trunk, your job is to figure out what connects all of these passion points in your life.

TURN PASSION INTO PURPOSE

Let's say that after connecting the dots on your map, noting everything that shares qualities and what those qualities are, you see that so much of what's on your map involves being outside. That's a great starting point! You'll probably need a life that keeps you outdoors a lot, because that has consistently sparked passion in you.

Or maybe you already know what some of your passions are, and you're not sure how to build a life around them. If you're passionate about skiing, for example—so much that you want to be an Olympic-level skier—there are some things you'd need to do. You would have to train constantly. You would have to move to a place known for skiing. You would have to factor in what's financially realistic, what's realistic for your family, and so on. That's one path that you could take.

Your Mind Map can reveal so much more.

As you scribble the things you love all over that pad of paper, you might see that you love to ski. You might also see you love to be outdoors, to hang out with groups of people, to take care of your dog, etc. The branches and connection points in your Mind Map can help you dig deeper, beyond what you thought your life *should* look like since you love skiing so much.

Skiing means being outside. It means being in the mountains. It means being in the recreational industry. It means traveling.

Suddenly, the branches have opened up new possibilities for you. What if you could create a life where you worked for Vail Resorts, doing sales and development for their corporate relations? You're in the ski industry, you're traveling, you're at resorts frequently. Your life is cool and fits right in line with your passions, even though it's not being an Olympic skier like you'd originally planned. It's partly how I ended up building a dog care empire. I thought I wanted to be a veterinarian. Until I took chemistry and biology, ha! I knew I loved hanging out with dogs. I knew I was entrepreneurial. I loved the idea of helping others build their own businesses around something they are passionate about. The pet industry was booming. The franchise industry was hot. Connect all those dots and voila—Camp Bow Wow!

DIP YOUR TOES IN

When you first make a map and start to identify passions, your next steps might not be obvious. It can sometimes take a little bit to get from Olympic skier to a more realistic path. Mapping lets us keep growing the branches until we see patterns and opportunities.

Before Camp Bow Wow, I fell into so many jobs and roles outside of my passions and strengths. I thought I knew what my life was going to be and tried to shape my choices around that. But years later, when I sold Camp Bow Wow and had to decide what came next, I took a completely different approach.

Everyone told me to just chill out, stay home with my kids, and enjoy the time. I looked at it completely differently. For the first time in fifteen years, I didn't have to worry about my business, my employees, and the franchisees, and could think about doing other things. The excitement quickly became paralyzing, though, with so many possibilities on the table.

I had to learn to enjoy it. I could start again, this time mapping out what would feel good, where opportunities might be, what I might want to try, and how I could explore without going all in. (This would have been so helpful earlier on in life!)

If you're thinking about being an astronaut, you don't have to jump right to a PhD program to make that happen. You might start by going to camp in Florida first. You might shadow an astronaut for a day—or several different kinds of astronauts! You might explore all the different jobs related to astronautical engineering and give them a try to see what resonates with your passions.

So many of us think in *all or nothing* terms, and that's what makes our passions seem unrealistic. We think, either I'm going to space or I'm not doing it at all. Either I'm working out like nobody's business all month or I'm staying on the couch. Instead, dip your toe in. Bring playfulness and joy back into your life and make it a game! Not being able to be an Olympic skier or the next person on the moon isn't the end of the world. Keep mapping and exploring until you can see what those interests and passions are pointing you toward.

TAKE IT A LAYER AT A TIME

It can also help to layer your Silhouette over the map

you create. Once you know what you're interested in and enjoy, look at it from the lens of your personality strengths. If you want to do something outdoors, and you're an Explorer who loves digging into data, what possibilities exist at that intersection? Who is living that type of life? Suddenly, you're seeing new opportunities, like geographic mapping for Google, that hadn't been on your radar before.

That added layer can move you from a generic life path to something fascinating that lets you live within your strengths and passions.

It's important to build up to this point, though, with your Silhouette and Mind-Mapped passions explored first. Your Silhouette comes first so that you can see how you roll—how you function as yourself, without any outside perspectives. Then you can explore your passions, but your only limitation should be that you're authentic to your personality and the things that make you tick. Hold off on the reality check until you've let yourself loose to dream, play, and explore.

With your passions mapped out, you can check it against reality to turn possibilities into opportunities. Look at what exists. See what other people are doing and what you can actually build a life around. Then let yourself ease into it. If everything you want to do involves sports and you know you want to be involved in that some way, somehow, even if you're just selling tickets at a Rockies game, then start by selling tickets at a Rockies game and see where that takes you.

Remember, though, that it's not anyone else's reality or expectations you're checking. This is still about building the life *you* want to live. When you're exploring ways to live your passion, check in with yourself on three things: attitude, ability, and alignment.

Make sure you're looking at things that you're drawn to with a great attitude—they line up with your Silhouette and you get excited about them. Look at what interests you, what you're aligned with, and think about why you want to do it and how you're approaching it. Then, of those things, look closer at what you've got an ability for—things that you're capable of making happen, with your own skills and training or something you can acquire.

If you have a great attitude about the concept of coding, that's one thing, but if you've really struggled with those skills and procrastinate learning them, it might not be a good choice. And then—and only then—make sure you've got the ability to turn it into an opportunity. If you've got the attitude and ability in place, we can work on getting you in the right job, with the right friends, and in the right relationship to make sure you're in alignment with your vision and values for your life.

IT'S ALL ABOUT YOU (IN THE BEST WAY)

I don't shout my map of what I'm doing to everybody. There are definitely times when people can't make sense of what I'm doing—this board over here, that initiative over there, a new company, or a new venture—when to me it makes perfect sense. That's because I know what I'm passionate about and can see how it connects. Everything I'm doing always ties back to my passions. But I don't shout it from the rooftops. I don't draw everyone a diagram, though it would make perfect sense to them if I did.

It's okay for other people to not get it. I get it.

One of the most important things you can do, especially when you get into high growth mode, is to set clear boundaries. I've struggled with this my entire life, whether it was with friends, boyfriends, work, or even family. Giving yourself space to stay focused and saying no when you need to is powerful. And not explaining yourself to everyone around you is just fine.

Too often, we feel like we have to justify a "no." We girls especially love to keep going until we've explained ourselves away. When someone tells us that we *should* do something, from going out on a Friday night to joining a board, it's so hard to just decline. We keep going with explanations, reasons, or justification, and it's exhausting. Learn to just say no and stop talking. No explanations, just no or no, thank you. It's so powerful!

Staying true to your vision, without getting knocked off of your course, is nothing short of bravery.

Your passion becomes your compass. By the end of this book, you'll have a plan of attack for any goal that you want to achieve, and it all comes back to creating a life that's aligned with who you are and what makes you jump out of bed in the morning. For example, you might be working on the SheFactor focus areas (we call them Spheres)—Faith, Fuel, and Finance. When someone tells you, "I want you to go to Vegas with me next month!" you can check in with your compass. That trip to Sin City will knock you off of your budget and your diet, so is it really worth taking? How far will it pull you away from this life of passion, fulfillment, and the goals you're working toward? When we gauge our opportunities against that compass of passion and goals, it becomes so much easier to say no and to play the game for the long-term result.

You might even find, like I did, that you need to make changes in the people you surround yourself with. If you hate to work out but know you need to, do you really want to hang out with people who are couch potatoes, too, so you can all sit on the sofa eating potato chips? Probably not. On the other hand, you probably don't want to hang out with a workout queen who doesn't do anything else either. The people to listen to are the ones who gently remind you to take a deep breath and refocus on the goals you set for yourself.

As we'll see in the next chapter, surrounding yourself with the best possible people can help you stay true to yourself, what you're good at and enjoy, and what you're passionate about. That way, when you're just starting out in a job or a field and have to do those things that fall outside of your skillset and passion, you're supported. With the right mentors and peers around you, you'll be able to navigate tough situations better and be more productive than when you're fighting against a peer group with opposite goals and motivation.

EMBRACE THE JOURNEY

Are you still feeling a little bit apprehensive about identifying your passions or the possibilities in front of you? It's okay. At one point, when I'd sold the company, my coach told me something that changed my perspective. She said, "You have a lot of different choices in front of you. It's okay to just push gently on some of those doors.

See what opens easily and what's more of a struggle. Start with the doors that open easier, because it's usually a sign that that's where you're supposed to go."

For a Dreamer and high achiever like me, that was news. I used to think you identify a *should* and then push until it happens. Being able to embrace the paths that were more clearly and simply open to me—simply because they aligned with my Silhouette and passion—changed the game.

Whatever you're thinking about—and I know at this stage in your life you have a *lot* to think about—if the struggle is too much, maybe those are roadblocks that the universe is placing in front of you. Use your intuition and trust yourself if you think you need to shift course a little bit.

You don't have to complain about it being hard. You don't have to be whiny about things not working out. Just recognize what's happening around you and advocate for yourself and the life you're creating. Once you've figured out that you don't like to do a certain part of the job, there's no need to attach emotion to it—now you know, and you can do what's necessary to build competence until you can work your way into a more fulfilling position.

That position might wind up looking very different than it does now. As you look at your opportunities for the future, the degree, trade, or past experience that you've earned can be a good place to start, but those things are not limiters. Your degree in geology might be almost complete before you realize that your original job path isn't what you thought it'd be. That doesn't mean you have to jump ship right now or that you wasted your time. Build around the experience you've gained until you've built the life you want—and you'll need to do this throughout your whole life!

Your problems are going to change. Your passions are going to look different. This isn't an exercise that you do once to find a passion and then stick with that for your entire life.

You're going to ebb and flow, and that's part of the fun of life! Discovering new things, approaching life with a sense of adventure, feeling the fear, and doing it anyway—these are the steps you take toward real success. Creating a life of passion is about knowing who you are and doing what you love, without holding on to any other expectations.

The life you want to build might go against the life you thought you were supposed to have. It might go against your parents' wishes or society's wishes, your boyfriend's wishes or your teachers' and coaches' wishes. But there's a reason I like to think of goals in terms of games: games are changeable. If you're playing a game that you thought you'd like, you don't have to keep playing it. You can change it. In the same way, you have the power to change your path any time you want to. All you need is the courage and energy to make the change. That confidence is what we're building here.

You can build whatever life you want, but you're going to have to work for it. It won't come to you on a silver platter. No one owes it to you. In fact, the world, society, and the universe are going to throw curveballs and will try to pull you off course. You have to recognize what you want and the path that you need to take to get there, and then you have to hold yourself to it. Advocating for yourself and teaching people how to treat you is hard—but it's even harder to know what you want and need in the first place.

I want to see you standing in that place of empowerment. I want you to choose yourself and honor yourself in your life path. I want you to make confident decisions and believe in who you are. The smaller goals and accomplishments that we'll work on in this book can help you build your confidence as you approach the bigger things in life. At the end of the day, it's a practice that only you can hold yourself to.

Before we can begin that practice, we have one more piece of the foundation to lay: your support system.

When courage is difficult, it helps to surround yourself with supportive influences. Find a SheFactor champion who can look at this with you from the outside, like my coach did for me. Without her advice, I never would have given myself the permission to make connections and pursue my passions. In the next chapter, we'll talk more about the importance of having people like her around you, cheering you on, and offering you a balanced perspective.

PAUSE AND PRACTICE

You know more about who you are—now it's time to think about what you want. Did you make a Mind Map as you worked through this chapter? If not, it's time to break out some paper. Go sit outside, away from screens, with a paper in hand, and start to daydream. Think about your past. Think about your hobbies. Think about days you've loved and futures you've dreamed about. Write all of those thoughts down until the branches of your tree start to connect. Join the conversation about passion, purpose, and potential with #myshefactor.

CHAPTER THREE

PEOPLE

YOU ARE WHO YOU SURROUND YOURSELF WITH

Starting your journey might seem overwhelming. Don't be afraid to take that first step—even just a baby one. Find a mentor and develop a core group of women to help connect you and collaborate with as you're on the path. Ask other women for help and advice. They'll be honored you did. Walk—or better yet, RUN—through doors that open. You never know what will be waiting for you on the other side.

—KRISTIN STROHM, FOUNDER AND PRESIDENT, STARBOARD GROUP; PRESIDENT AND CEO, COMMON SENSE POLICY ROUNDTABLE

My first experience in choosing people to help me grow Camp Bow Wow didn't go well. One of my good friends was working in franchising at the time, and that was the next phase for Camp Bow Wow. I trusted her, and the business was growing quickly, so I agreed. She took on the operations side of things while I worked on sales and development.

At the same time, my grandfather became ill and passed away, so I moved to California to be close to my grandmother. Unfortunately, the whole time I was gone, my friend was siphoning money out of the accounts. She used the company to pay for lunches, furniture, and anything else that she wanted.

I knew something was off, but believe it or not, it took me some time to figure out exactly what it was. She denied all of it, to the point where I had to get the DA involved. The first time I hired a partner, it ended in me firing one of my best friends and bringing the DA in to get back the equity I'd given her as incentive.

Later, when I started to hire C-level people, I went through a string of executives that just didn't work out. Before I sat down with my coach, whom we talked about in the last chapter, I had started blaming myself.

Since then, I've come to love the saying "When people show you who they are, believe them—the first time." Learning the personality Silhouettes helped me to see what people were saying about themselves better. It helped me to trust my gut and learn to say no more (and with more conviction). It helped me to become more forgiving, not just of others, but also of myself for mis-reading people.

Personal responsibility is at the core of everything I wished that I'd learned and everything I hope you get from this book. As much as you can take responsibility for your own goals and actions to meet those goals, you *can* take responsibility for the people you bring into your life and the expectations you put on them. But at the same time, this isn't about you becoming a doormat. It's doling your trust out slowly, carefully choosing the people who will be influences in your life, and then teaching them how to treat you.

HIRE SLOW, FIRE FAST

Actions will always speak louder than words, and that's where people tell us who they really are. I always want to believe the best in people, but that has often left me explaining away bad behavior. *They didn't mean to...they didn't understand what I was asking...they didn't know...* Part of that comes from avoiding conflict. So many of us are afraid of having critical conversations, so it's easier to believe that the person had good intentions and just screwed up.

Sadly, this can go pretty far. *They only cheated on me once...*

If someone is late the first time they meet you, what are the chances that they're habitually late to everything? In those moments when someone shows us who they are, we have the ability to either give them more chances or to recognize who they are. You don't have to cut them off at the knees, but you can be a little slower to offer them trust.

It's so much easier now for me to look back at my twenty-year-old self and think, "Oh, my gosh—why did I date that guy? I saw it coming and just didn't believe it..." I wish I could have helped that version of me to be a bit more wary. I went into life giving the people around me a long leash, then pulling them back in when things got out of hand. I would give them all my trust right away, and when I needed to pull back, they wouldn't like it. They could feel that I was taking my trust away, and it would make them unhappy and rebellious.

The better way to do it is to start off with only little bits of trust that can grow over time. It's the principle of hiring slow and firing fast. Take time to let someone prove themselves, and believe them if they show you they aren't a person who deserves space in your life.

Your emotional intelligence and intuition are still growing, and I suppose on some level we learn by experience. But you can still trust those parts of you that raise the red flags and give yourself a voice. Your intuition speaks softly but carries a big stick.

UNDERSTAND YOURSELF, APPRECIATE OTHERS

Starting with the Silhouettes alone puts you ahead of a majority of the population in terms of emotional intelligence. We all naturally operate in a certain way. Asking someone to not be themselves isn't good for either party. If you're asking a Dreamer type to do data analysis in front of a computer all day, then they don't wind up doing a great job, whose fault is that? Or, if you get into a relationship with a Director who is rebellious and doesn't want to be boxed in, what's going to happen if you ask them to get married, have kids, and work an eight-to-five job in corporate America?

When it comes to the people around us, we have to be able to ask for what we need. That means teaching people how to treat us, as well as asking for support. For example, my friend Bree will send me fourteen-paragraph emails late at night. When she hits send, she feels great about the information she gave me and how she presented it. It gets it off her chest. She feels like she told me exactly what I need to know and that we should be able to move forward the next morning when I get it.

Unfortunately, my mornings are crazy. I'm running around in a million directions. Lunch boxes, homework in backpacks, dog barking…There's no way I can process that kind of information! I can't operate in that way. The closest I can come is to print her emails out and highlight what she's trying to say later in the day when I have a quiet moment (does that EVER happen?). That's the only way my bullet-point-sized brain can get through it.

"Bree," I try to remind her, "I need you to just send me one-liners and bullet points."

When that doesn't work for her, we get on a call and go over the information live—and quickly. That's the way we have to work together, because we need such very different types of written communication.

A lot of the work we're doing is meant to help you find your voice, so you can ask for what you need—whether it's from the universe, your boss, or your best friend. Asking for what you need can show up at work, like when Bree and I have to figure out how to communicate with each other. Or it can show up on a night out, when you ask your best friend to not let you take your credit card out.

This is a practice. Take every opportunity to grow that confidence in yourself, even when it gets messy. Find your voice and use it.

CREATE BETTER WORKPLACE DYNAMICS

At this point in your career, you won't be able to pick the perfect boss or choose the ideal work environment. Still, you can be cognizant of the dynamics you're walking into when you're interviewing for a position. Once we have that down for ourselves, we can recognize it in other people. We can see when they're outside of their strengths and passions, or when their Silhouettes just mean they operate differently than we do, and that can help us work with them in more efficient ways.

If the boss is super detail-oriented and that is a difficult personality for you to interact with, you can have some advance knowledge about the challenges you might face there. That doesn't mean you won't take the job, necessarily, but you'll know going in that this person is going to be a taskmaster, not a supportive, lovey-dovey person in your life.

Start to look at the people around you in terms of Silhouettes to see what you can learn about them. Someone who carries a lot of confidence and likes to be at the center of attention, without conforming to rules, is probably a Director. The person who's got the energy of a terrier and is all about getting stuff done is likely a Conqueror. When you see a daydreaming idealist trying to cure cancer, it's not hard to know you're talking to a Dreamer. (Side note: if you're in an interview and want to get an idea of who you'll be working for, ask them questions! *If I work for you, how should I report my progress and how often? How do you like to interact with your staff? What are some things your favorite team members do? What things do your team members do that upset you?*)

The next step is to pay attention to the ways those types interact. Dreamers are visionary, big thinkers, while Directors are project oriented and like to have a lot going on without being boxed in. When those two get together, the Director looks up to the Dreamer, who is able to see a bigger picture outside of the creative boxes that the Director bounces between. Meanwhile, the Dreamer respects the Director's ability to be feisty, clever, and to say no, which is counter to the inspirational, loving, inclusive persona that the Dreamer has.

Not all types work so well together, though everyone can respect the strengths that someone else has. We Dreamers admire the Explorer's ability to parse out data, though we don't have as much envy for that ability as we might for a Storyteller's ability to articulate. Each Silhouette has their gift, and while we don't necessarily want to give our gifts up for someone else's, we often admire and respect other people for their own, once we learn how they work.

This isn't a new concept—people who are familiar with astrology know what to expect when Virgos and Leos get together. A lot of those are stereotypes, but we're drawn to them because we like to have everything in nice little boxes. Silhouettes can be approached in the same way. If you're an Explorer dating a Dreamer, you can have a good idea of the types of conflicts you're going to bump up against. You don't have to become a psychological genius about Silhouettes and personality traits but having it on your radar might just make your life a little bit easier.

Knowing what you need can also mean knowing what you *don't* need. *The E-Myth* and *The E-Myth Revisited*, both by Michael Gerber, talk about this concept in the context of a pie shop. If a pie shop has a baker, someone at the front desk, and a manager, even if the shop is small, that doesn't mean the roles are interchangeable. The baker won't be an intuitively good manager. The manager won't be as intuitively good at sales behind the front desk. And no matter how good your baker is, you can't assume that promoting them into sales would lead to success.

This is probably where we got the business wisdom "sales people don't make good sales managers." Unfortunately, that's not wisdom we follow. What's the first thing companies try to do when someone is doing a great job? We try to promote them into management positions. Those lifestyles and motivations are so very different, but we're somehow surprised when it doesn't work out.

Sometimes promotions and job openings are tempting when they have those external markers of success. But if they're not in your wheelhouse, if they're not something you're passionate about, you're not going to thrive. Even if saying no means you have to give up the salary and the company car, like I did when I left pharmaceutical sales, none of those markers are worth being miserable. If we can start by recognizing these traits and preferences in ourselves—are you the field person or the manager at the desk?—then we can learn to say *no* and stick to our goals.

LEVEL UP YOUR INTERPERSONAL INTERACTIONS

At Camp Bow Wow, we had to have a working knowledge of dog training. The way you get a dog to behave well is to reinforce good behavior with treat after treat, time and time again. When they do something wrong, you redirect them back to the right behavior—you don't kick them or punish them.

As sad as it sounds, this is not unlike the way we can teach people to treat us better. You can find your voice and stand up for yourself. It's so important to articulate what feels right in a relationship and what doesn't and see how they respond. With positive and clear directions, we can often break down some of the conflict that makes these conversations so scary. And BE consistent.

For example, instead of complaining about your boy-friend to your own friends, try the "two positives for every negative" approach. Tell him, "I'm so glad you asked me out on a date night! The restaurant was great. And I know you don't have to be on time every time—I get that's how you roll—but it's different for me. When you're late, it changes how I feel about things and how I see our relationship. It would mean a lot to me if you could make an effort to be on time."

Over time, keep reminding him that when he's late, it feels like he's disrespecting your time or doesn't want to be with you. Verbalize how it feels. In counseling, they teach us to use *I* statements to demonstrate how we're feeling—*I feel disappointed when you show up late*, instead of *You're always late*.

You can even go a step further to help him find a solution: "Can you tell me you'll be there thirty minutes later than you plan to be so that I'm not left waiting?"

He may still not think it's a big deal. But if you never told him, he'd never know. Keep telling him. Never stop speaking up for yourself. You are your best advocate. This is why we took the time to figure ourselves out first and get clear on the things that make us tick. If you don't know who you are, how are you going to be able to tell anyone else? People don't know what you need automatically, and it's not their responsibility to figure it out. It's yours. It's up to you to teach them how to treat you.

And it's up to you to treat yourself well, too.

Instead of focusing on things you're doing wrong, celebrate what's going right. And as long as you're taking baby steps toward your goals, there's no bad score anyway. Slow progress is better than no progress. Be kind to yourself on this journey, and only save space for the people in your life who will learn to treat you well.

YOUR SHEFACTOR SEAL TEAM

As you focus your life around your goals and get clear on what you need and how people should treat you, a handful of people will elevate themselves above the rest. You'll intuitively build stronger relationships with people who align with what you're trying to do in life. Of course, there will always be people in our proximity who aren't our biggest supporters, but we don't have to give everyone the same trust and place in our lives.

I call that closest inner circle my SheFactor SEAL Team.[2] A little like the badasses in the military, they always have your back.

---

2   Thanks, Harris Faulkner, for inspiring me with your SEAL Team 6 idea!

These are the people who love you and support you. They know what you're trying to accomplish and will help you get there. It's a small circle, because when you're working toward goals, it's hard to keep a close relationship with very many people. There are usually just a handful of standouts that make the cut.

Think for a minute about the five or six most important people in your life right now. Some longtime friends or family members might be on the list. There's your best friend that knows you inside and out, or your mom who you talk to every day.

Maybe you've just moved to a new city after graduating, and someone at work really clicks with you. You're always going to her for advice, and if you were going to trust anyone at work, it'd be her.

You might go work out with a group of friends once a week, and one of them in particular stands out to you. You look up to her and feel comfortable deferring to her on things surrounding food and fitness in your life.

There might be a church group leader who was part of your groups in high school and college, and you've stayed friends. Every few weeks, you go to coffee together. Their advice has always been something you respect and honor, and they are always supportive of you.

Your SEAL Team is reserved for the people who know what you're trying to accomplish, know how you're trying to get there, and are completely supportive of that process. You feel inspired by them and know that they care about you like nobody's business. Your best interests come first, and you can trust them in that. Honestly, you might wind up with the guy who works at the front door of your apartment building in this circle. If they've proven that they're on your team no matter what, there are no rules around where that relationship has to start.

If your brother is against everything you're doing in this phase of life, he's not part of your SEAL Team. You still love him and will listen to what he has to say, but you're not aligned. Your team comes with a powerful feeling of connection and support.

SURROUND YOURSELF WITH IMPECCABLE PEOPLE

One of the most important things you can do is to surround yourself with the right people—folks who have your back no matter what, who make you feel inspired, encouraged, cared about, and loved. Having the right people to lean on will solve so many other problems in your life. Think of it like *The Office*. Those people had some of the most miserable jobs, but they played off each other, leaned on each other, and created a great story.

On the other hand, if you're around people who don't share your goals or vision and who don't support you on your path in life, you'll lose motivation. Letting those people be a voice in your ear is exhausting. If you're not aligned in your close relationships, it becomes easier to ignore the instinct that tells us to step away and instead follow emotions until we're dragged away from our goals.

Your instincts are smart. Instincts are the quiet, steady, contemplative voice inside of you that knows what's right and wrong. They know when you shouldn't be with someone or when you shouldn't listen to advice and direction. Emotions live on the surface and tell you, *it's okay; it'll work out; it's too hard to be alone so just make it work*. Emotions don't care about you or what's good for you in the long term.

Sometimes, well-meaning influences in our lives have a similar short-term focus. Run everything through your own instincts first. When someone gives you advice, first consider whether they are part of your SEAL Team or if they're outside of that circle. Then think about what's in it for them. For example, if they're coming from a place of worry, that's an emotion connected to fear. They won't want you to take a risk.

As I grew into my instincts and began to trust myself instead of buying into fear, I learned to connect with people in much deeper, more effective ways. Most recently, when I ran my campaign for CU regent, those fears started to creep up again.

There was a dear friend that I wanted to hire to help me run my campaign, and when I looked at my past experience through a lens of fear, I was sure it wouldn't work. *I don't know how to do this. I can't hire friends or family. I have to defer to someone else to make this decision.*

When I took a deep breath and looked at the bigger picture, things changed. I asked myself what skillset I needed for the campaign. I thought about what Silhouette would work best with mine. When I took our friendship out of the equation, I found that she really did fit. Perfectly. So my next question was, *am I brave enough to try this again?* Could I use everything I'd learned to make it right this time?

We were both totally committed to both the process *and* to not screwing up our friendship. We were hell-bent on being open and honest with each other. We're politically on the same side, which helped. While she'd never worked on a political campaign in her life, neither had I. We'd worked in similar industries and knew each other really well, so we decided to have fun figuring this out together. And we were tenacious and stubborn enough to do this thing that no one thought we could do, especially without any political experience.

While that early experience at Camp Bow Wow hiring a friend turned out to be one of the worst work experiences of my life, working with Jill became one of the best. I'd learned how to pick impeccable people, how to slow down in offering trust, and how to interact with others more thoughtfully. As you'll see in the chapters to come, those were hard-earned lessons. Learn all you can from the people around you so that you'll have less to work through on your own. Build that foundation of a strong personality that you own, a clear passion to focus on, and impeccable people that you can lean on—and the rest will fall into place.

PAUSE AND PRACTICE

In the next half of the book, we're going to work on your goals, focusing on categories of things where day-to-day life actually happens. Having your personality, passion, and people in clear focus will make the rest of the book that much more effective. You've already identified your personality type (your Silhouette) and mapped out your passion. Now it's time to identify your SEAL Team. It's okay if you don't have it down just yet. Write down some possibilities, and we'll work more on interpersonal relationships in the next chapter. Join the conversation about the people in our lives and how they build us up or hold us back with #myshefactor.

PART II

FUTURE FIERCE: USING SHEFACTOR SPHERES TO TRACK FOR SUCCESS

CHAPTER FOUR

FOLK

OPTIMIZING RELATIONSHIPS WITH FRIENDS, FAMILY, AND FR-AMILY

Happiness is having a large, loving, caring, close-knit family—in another city.

—GEORGE BURNS

All throughout my early life, I had family members who were my biggest supporters. From the time I was young, my mom and dad believed I could do anything, and they imparted that confidence in me. My dad coached me in soccer when we lived in California (from the time I was six!), and when we moved to Colorado, there wasn't a place for me to play, so my parents started the first little chapter of the American Youth Soccer Organization in our town. It spread all over the state. That community organizing effort by our family is how I got my full-ride scholarship and wound up at SMU.

When I lost my scholarship and my dad lost his job, they supported me as I moved out to California, where my grandparents took me in. Through all my ups and downs to finish school, my family continued to be supportive when I wound up back in California working as a receptionist for an ad agency out of college. It wasn't the most glamorous of jobs, but it was in a field that I loved. And when I needed something new after my move back to Colorado a couple years later, it was my dad who helped me find a job in pharmaceutical sales.

The people closest to us shape us in so many ways, and for me that was very much my family and some close friends. It'd be fantastic to only interact with people on that level. To raise the bar to the SEAL Team—people who are always supportive and motivated toward our best interests. We all know, though, that's not reality. How, then, do we optimize those relationships that take a little bit more work? As with everything else, it starts with us.

We have to break down our biases about who we are (like we did in the first part of this book) and who the people around us are until the canvas is clean and we can learn to understand each other better.

BREAK THE HABITS

In the last chapter, we talked a lot about teaching others how to treat us. An important piece of that is giving them that same courtesy. The Golden Rule never gets old: "Treat others as you would have them treat you."

When we struggle in relationships, it's often because of the assumptions we're bringing to the situation. We might see someone as coming to work grumpy, difficult, and not following through with their projects. But what if they just had a big fight with their boyfriend and have brought that stress with them? Assuming will always get us in trouble. Coming from a place of empathy rather than judgment can help us shed those assumptions and start to treat the people around us with the same respect and thoughtfulness that we want from them.

Thoughtfulness comes from a place of intention, while assumptions come from a place of habit. We get into habits in our relationships—in fact, some of our relationships are habitual in themselves. We stop trying to move that relationship forward and start settling for our assumptions, habits, and ruts.

Think about a relationship with recurring fights. We all have them. You might always argue with your significant other about spending too much money, or you might always argue with your mom about the same thing. To break out of that habit, you have to look deeper:

- Why do you always fight about that?

- What causes that fight?

- How do you shift that dynamic?

- What's another perspective you can look at it from?

- Can you try something new next time it feels like a fight is coming?

The first step in any relationship is to build some empathy for that person. What are their motivations, separate from the assumptions you've made about them? If someone is always getting defensive or overwhelmed when you have big ideas, maybe they're coming from a place of fear. Maybe they feel overrun by you and need to be validated and appreciated as a leader in their own right.

If you can identify that motivation, then make a decision to approach that situation from an angle of empathy, you'll start to break out of assumptions and bad habits. You'll start to solve the puzzle and build a more productive relationship.

The recurring theme of *choice* starts here with the focus area Folk and will continue in every single area of life. When you let your life just happen to you, you'll wind up on someone else's path. You'll have someone else's relationships and habits, someone else's ideal career, and someone else's life. You're here because you want more—because you want your own life.

It's hard to think about choice when it comes to friends and family. Our family members seem to be a forced relationship. (*That's just my family. It's just how they are!*) Often, our friend groups feel set as well. (*Squad goals!*) But we have the same level of choice with Folk as we do in any other category. Let's look at the responsibilities we have to choose the relationships that we cultivate, the way we interact in those relationships, and when it's time to let go of a relationship.

INTENTIONAL RELATIONSHIPS

Being intentional about who we let into our lives first means knowing what we're looking for. In a perfect world, what does a great relationship with a boyfriend, boss, or friend look like to you?

My relationship with Bion, my first husband, was really good. And I love my relationship with Jason, my husband of ten years, so much. But in between, I went through a string of bad boyfriends. After divorcing Tori's dad, I raised my daughter alone for about ten years. Two guys in particular just didn't treat me well—not in an abusive way, but not respectful or appreciative either. So, after the dust settled from those two bad actors, I stepped back and made a list. I wrote down all of the attributes that would make me feel great about the next person I might be in a relationship with. It sounds a little silly at first, and today I like to joke about it; while I did make a list that helped me find my husband, Jason, I left a few things off, like cleaning up his closet. Joking aside, things like honesty, ambition, and a love of college football (yes, really) showed up on that list and showed up strong when I started dating Jason.

In fact, I mentioned the list to my good friend Becca, and that's what triggered her to set us up on a blind date. She told me a cute young guy had just moved in next door to her, and since we both liked sports (which she did NOT), we were destined to meet. Our third date was to the Rockies–Red Sox World Series game in '07, and we had so much fun we got kicked out of the club section for being too rowdy. It was meant to be.

Whether it's coincidence or not, the list of attributes I was looking for described Jason pretty darn well. Perhaps the universe just needed me to get my act together and figure out what I wanted in a partner (and write it down) before landing me at Centro in Boulder on that blind date.

When I met Bion, my first husband, I was in a similar state of mind. I'd been through a rash of not-so-hot relationships and was ready to change up my approach to dating. I was reminded what I was NOT looking for in order to find what I was. Once I got clear about the traits that were important to me, I met the man that I would marry.

If you can shake off the feeling of making a grocery list for humans, this exercise has very real value. I wanted someone I could trust completely. Someone who was loyal. Someone who could make me laugh. We all have those top four or five things that turn us into mush in a romantic relationship or make us feel safe and appreciated in friendships and at work. When you can get them on paper—really think through what they are, identify them, and see them in one place—you can start to recognize them in the people around you. Maybe, more importantly, you will start to notice when the relationships in your life don't meet those standards. It's a first step in teaching people how to treat you—and, equally, making sure you treat them just as well.

When you start to speak up for yourself in your relationships, people will be confused at first. They might not realize they weren't being affectionate enough or that taking out the trash in the morning means so much to you. Chances are, anyone in a healthy relationship will want to make you happy. It just might take some mirroring—treating them how you want to be treated—and reminding them what's important to you in order to make it happen, then celebrating with them when they get it right!

If they don't have any interest in respecting those

requests, however, that's a pretty big red flag. The thing is, you're not obligated to remain in a close relationship with anyone. In the last chapter, we talked about the importance of your SEAL Team and the people who earn your trust. All too often, we feel obligated to offer similar levels of trust to people outside of that circle.

If you're not happy with your relationships, it's time to take some action and intentionally engage in that process. Think about the relationships you do want, where you'll meet those people, and what you need to do to get that process in motion. Put yourself in situations where you can help your existing relationships up their game or where you can meet people who will form relationships that you want.

INTENTIONAL PERSPECTIVE

There are some relationships that exist in our lives whether we want them to or not. We can't always choose our bosses or our parents, for example. Teachers and coworkers aren't always flexible either. Perspective is important for all of our relationships, but it's especially important in the relationships that we're obligated to.

In these cases, we can choose to take an active role in those relationships. We can advocate for ourselves and articulate what we need, and we can put energy into more appropriate, effective relationships that balance out the time and energy spent in more draining ways. There are also going to be seasons of ups and downs with people. Sometimes, you'll need your mom desperately. Other times, you'll talk to her every other week and be fine.

You don't have to get rid of everybody, even if you're surrounded by unhealthy relationships. Start to build the relationships that you want and need in your life, and the people who are unwilling to grow with you will fall off naturally.

We can also practice having healthier conflicts, so that relationships that are a struggle don't get stuck in unproductive cycles. This isn't easy. Conflict is a case where we have to *feel the fear—and do it anyway*. If you don't deal with tough conversations right when they need to happen, you'll just postpone it, harboring the feelings until it comes back up again. Be brave. Be willing to face those conversations, especially when they're small, before they build to something bigger. Feel the fear—and do it anyway.

Addressing more of these conflicts helps us gain a better perspective. It's much more productive to recognize that I'm not upset about my husband changing the channel when I was watching a show—I'm upset about feeling disrespected. I'm wondering if he cares about my happiness in everyday life.

That can help us look deeper into the other person's motivation as well. If my boss complains about a report that I've written, can I look deeper to find the reason they're complaining? Is it because they're afraid of being blamed for my bad report? Or do they worry that I won't be able to do the job they need me to do? When we take a deep breath and step back far enough to see what's really going on, we can address it more directly.

If I can say, "Time-out—you changed the channel when I was watching my show, and I feel totally disrespected right now. That wasn't cool," we can deal with that pretty quickly. Those small, silly things that tick us off provide a great way to practice for the bigger things.

When we deal with conflicts as they arise, even though it's a form of conflict that we'd rather avoid, it also helps us avoid bigger conflicts. If he changes the channel several times in a row and I hold that frustration in, it might bubble up and show up all of a sudden in the subway or in the store when another conflict sets it off. Suddenly, "I'm feeling disrespected right now" turns into "You *always*" and "You *never*," which blocks productive conversation.

In the book *The Four Agreements,* one of the agreements is that your word is impeccable. You are bound by the words that come out of your mouth, so be very careful when you choose them. They will leave an impact on the person you're talking to—sometimes, on the whole world— regardless of your intention. I learned this while running my campaign and speaking in front of crowds every day (and to the media). Words really do matter. Choosing them well so that, as much as possible, you can't be mis- understood, is a skill that you can practice every single day. Everything that comes out of your mouth, everything that you post on social media, everything that you com- municate should be considered carefully. I've learned the lesson over and over; words matter.

You can have tough conversations all day long. To find them and approach them well, be conscientious of your interactions with people, what you need, and where they're coming from. By practicing on smaller conflicts, we're better prepared when something actually does grow to be a bigger heart conversation and a more dif- ficult situation to navigate. Your confidence in who you are, the topic at hand, and your ability to handle the con- versation usually determines whether that conversation will go badly.

LETTING GO WITH INTENTION

One of my best friends—someone I have been best buddies with since I was three months old (really—our moms were next-door neighbors)—is completely on the opposite side of the political spectrum from me. We're still best friends. We adore each other! But we have to be careful about letting conversations veer off into that territory. You can probably relate, as many of us are dealing with this right now. We'll talk more about having open and meaningful conversations on this topic in chapter 7, Freedom, but there are definitely cases where you just have to let it go.

Emotional intelligence and those instincts we're learning to trust can tell us when we need to have conflict and when it's time to let something go. You have to pick and choose your battles and let go of things that won't be productive. A good indication is the cost of the conflict.

Will this conversation come with collateral damage? Is that worth it for a conversation about politics or what time your kids should go to bed or whether your boyfriend called you when he was going to be late? Sometimes it is. Sometimes it isn't. The skills you're building around knowing yourself and the other person, looking deeper at motivations and the underlying problem, and implementing that Golden Rule will help you make that decision.

We're often fearful of tough conversations because we know they're going to cost something. We have a good idea of how they're going to go. Most of us won't fight with our significant others in the first six months of a relationship because we don't want to mess anything up.

That's why we've got to build that critical conversation muscle, like we talked about in chapter 3.

REWIND AND REFLECT

Struggling to know what to do in a tough conversation? You don't always have to respond right away. Practice these conflict skills to help you make clear-headed decisions:

- "Let me think about that."

- "I need to sit on that for a few minutes."

- "Can we take a time-out and talk about that in ten minutes?"

- "I need to put my thoughts together."

Taking a pause to breathe is one of the most impactful things you can do in difficult situations!

Sometimes, we can attempt clear communication and healthy conflict over and over without the relationship improving. If you go back to the intuition questions we asked about our relationships (how does it make you feel, is it healthy, is it encouraging? etc.) and find that you're answering no more often than not, then your energy might be better spent elsewhere.

Again, this doesn't mean you have to end the relationship. But you can give yourself a break. That might look like taking a break, not talking as much, or pulling back some of the energy you put into your interactions. Give yourself that space, and then check in to see how that feels. If you take a break for a week or two and really miss that person and need to be with them, it'll be clear that the relationship is worth working on from a different angle.

Your energy is such a precious resource. You only have so many dollars in the bank. You only have so many minutes in the day. And you only have so much energy to put out into the universe.

Without getting too far out there, it's important to visualize these tender souls that we all have. Be protective of yourself. Be careful about who you let in and give access to that space. If you're taking in someone else's negative energy or funneling all of your energy to someone who is going to do damage, you have to take responsibility for that.

Part of the game of life is figuring out how you can spend that time, money, and energy. As you work on the categories we're focusing on, when you spend in one category, it'll take from what you have available for the others. If you put all of your energy into pleasing your boss, it will cost something in another area of your life. You don't get more than 100 percent. Think hard about where that line is for you.

Choose wisely when it comes to who you'll give that

energy to. Choose who you let in and who you want to impact that precious soul of yours. Set boundaries, make good decisions, and be strong in your "yes" and your "no." You don't have to just let life happen to you. You don't have to let everyone in. You don't have to drain your finite resources to people who aren't going to give anything back.

When that feels intimidating or lonely, turn back to your SEAL Team and your champion—your mentor. You have people in your corner, and we all want to see you win.

PAUSE AND PRACTICE

So much of our lives can be lost to dead-end relationships and people pleasing. For this chapter, we're going to have a two-part exercise. Start with your SheFactor SEAL Team that you've identified, plus anyone else that you spend a significant amount of time with. Write down as much as you can about them—their names, your best guess at their Silhouette, who they are to you, what they do in their own life, how happy and optimistic they are in their own lives, how they support you. Note whether or not you have any obvious gaps—types of support that are missing, relationships that you know you need to cultivate, end, etc.

Now, for the next week, keep a diary of your interactions with those people. Start asking for what you need in everyday life, practice those small but challenging conversations, and see what happens. What kind of reactions do those people have? At the end of the week, see if you have any changes to your assessment of people—your SEAL Team might even change! Chime in with your surprises and aha moments during this exercise with #myshefactor.

CHAPTER FIVE

FLAME

YOUR SIGNIFICANT OTHER SHOULD BE A BRIGHT LIGHT IN YOUR LIFE

Before you marry a person, you should first make them use a computer with slow Internet service to see who they really are.

—WILL FERRELL

The day after high school graduation, I met a guy at the local lake where we all hung out in Monument. He'd graduated three years before me and was going to school at the University of Southern Colorado in Pueblo, but we shared a group of friends. Even though I was headed off to SMU in Texas, we fell in love and got serious—fast.

For three years, we dated. I wound up bouncing from

Texas to California, and he lived with me for a little bit. He also moved to South Korea for an assignment and did some other big traveling as a journalist in the Army. Like I said, we were really serious—until he married someone else. While we were still dating.

That's a story for a later chapter (I promise), because why and how it happened isn't really the point here. It's how much that rocked me to the core. I didn't know how I'd missed the signs—why didn't I know it was coming? In response, I got into a bit of a rebellious streak. For a couple of years, I wasn't taking care of myself, I partied a lot, and I dated some questionable characters.

After college, and two years in California, I moved back to Colorado and briefly dated someone I'd known since I was younger. There wasn't a lot there—we were friends more than anything. But he dumped me on the same day that my good friend was dumped, and we were ticked. We went to a club in downtown Denver, completely mad at ALL guys, determined to never date again.

And then he showed up.

Weirdly, I was smoking the only cigarette I'd ever smoked in my life, completely angry and upset...and these two guys walked up to ask us to dance. Sorry—two *reallllly good-looking* guys asked us to dance. One of them was

Bion, who later became my first husband, and the other wound up marrying my friend.

Bion loved me exactly as I was, without expecting anything different from me. He adored me. There was no wondering how he felt or what the agenda was. In fact, he told me that the only turn-off for him the night we met was that I was smoking. (That one cigarette, that one time. Whoops!) Our whole relationship was so comfortable, honest, and open. He supported my dreams and encouraged me in them. In fact, Camp Bow Wow started out as a business plan that he and I sketched out on a napkin at the local Mexican restaurant. He was my best friend, and I'd never known anything like it before.

His sudden death ripped my heart out.

I'd finally found this person—I finally knew what love was supposed to be like—and it was just...gone. *He* was gone.

I decided that the only logical answer was that I had never deserved him in the first place. He was too good to be true.

Months after he died, I went to my ten-year high school reunion and ran into the guy who would become the father of my oldest, Tori. I'd known him since seventh grade (actually, it was his twin brother who dumped me the night I met Bion), and I knew he'd been in a bit of trouble the last couple years with drinking. But it didn't matter. I wanted some kind of normal so badly that I justified the relationship in spite of all the red flags.

Our relationship should have stayed as friends; it wasn't fair to him, or to me, how it played out. I was still very in love with Bion and reeling from his sudden death. He was still struggling with drugs and alcohol and searching for his own kind of normal. I recall my grief counselor telling me, "Go ahead and enjoy spending time with your old friend, but whatever you do, DON'T GET MARRIED AND DON'T GET PREGNANT!"

Guess what I did? Both. We cared for each other in the way that you care for someone you've known for so long. He was one of my best friends in high school. But we just couldn't stay married with all the trauma we brought into it.

When he and I split up, I was completely convinced I'd never deserved the one good relationship I'd had, and I wasn't sure I deserved a good relationship at all. Maybe part of me didn't want to be in love that way again because of how badly it had hurt to lose Bion. After so many abrupt endings, I had the sense that the rug could be pulled out from under me at any time. I couldn't completely trust good things because they *must* be too good to be true, and I couldn't completely trust good people because all of those love letters from Korea must not have meant anything after all.

Ultimately, I stopped trusting myself, too.

The guys I dated after losing Bion (and my marriage to Tori's dad) were really good-looking and seemed to have it together on the outside, but inside, they were insecure jerks. I oscillated between too much commitment too quickly and never really trusting anyone at all. Maybe if I'd been brave enough to trust myself, I could have ended the bad relationships and looked for something better.

Our time is precious—*your* time is so precious. I hope you'll let me be an outspoken friend for you in this chapter, so that you can go on to make braver choices than I did.

DO YOU TRUST YOUR PARTNER?

When you were little, did your parents tell you that trust was like a bank? You put coins into the bank to develop trust over time, and when someone makes a withdrawal from that account, it takes a long time to build it back up.

Usually, we're still in that relationship while we try to build it up, too. It can happen around money, it can happen around cheating—trust can be broken in so many ways. If you continue the relationship after they say something like "I was drinking—it means nothing! I love you and want to be with you!" look at the dynamics of the relationship. Those dynamics will change after a betrayal.

When trust is broken, you're always looking, always wondering, always unsure of whether you can believe what they're telling you. You become defensive in interactions and wary about what they're telling you. Then that person senses the wall and gets angry that you won't trust them. It's a nasty cycle that we get caught up in, sometimes without even realizing it's happening.

Fear can keep us in relationships we shouldn't be in as well. It's hard enough to start over in a new relationship, much less find someone in the first place, so it's easy to tell ourselves that the person we're with has "potential." Some of us are confident enough to say, "The first time someone shows me who they are, I'm out of here." Then there's the rest of us.

Maybe it's insecurity. Maybe it's wanting to believe the best in people. At the end of the day, though, we have to prioritize what's good for us, what's feeding our souls, and what we're going to tolerate. Holding to that line can create confidence in itself, which will exude to the people we're in relationships with. Ironically, that confidence often affects how they treat us and what they think they can get away with.

Some of us do find that, with time and maturity, it becomes easier to see the red flags more clearly. We can get past the starry eyes of a new relationships faster to see when someone isn't going to work out.

Different Silhouettes handle relationship problems in different ways. A rebellious Director might cheat on someone who cheated on her. She'll definitely be inclined to be feisty about conflict. A Dreamer tends to get lost in the potential of how romantic and wonderful the relationship could be—more in love with the idea of the relationship than the person. A Conqueror might be more likely to force a less-than-ideal relationship because it's what she's "supposed" to be doing in her life right now.

Similarly, trying to control a Director in a relationship is a bad idea. Giving a Dreamer a chore list isn't going to go well. Each personality pairing will have its own dynamics and will love—and fight—in different ways.

Remember "hire slow, fire fast?" That shows up over and over again in our lives, from friendships to careers to romantic relationships. You don't owe anyone trust right away. In fact, you owe it to yourself to slow way down. Interview the heck out of potential partners, even though it's not a literal interview. Get to know people incredibly well before you give those pieces of your soul to them.

Did you catch the empowerment in my word choices

there? You have just as much control and power to choose in romantic relationships as in any other facet of your life. Why would some other person get to decide whether you're going out or not? Why would some guy determine whether you're ready to get married? You get to choose what you do with every second of your life—including whether or not you even want to be in a relationship. Use that power to bring people into your life who respect you, appreciate you, and care about who you are and where you're going in life. Hire slow and fire fast.

DO YOU TRUST YOUR TEAM?

Every girl knows that feeling—the one where your best friend gets a new boyfriend, then she suddenly disappears. It's not a great feeling, even if it's somewhat natural. It'll happen again when you and your friends start to have kids. You almost always wind up abandoning a certain subset of your friends, then when your kids are a little bit older, you look around and wonder where your friends went. No one really means for it to happen or even likes it. It happens because of that finite amount of time we talked about in chapter 4.

If you've developed your SEAL Team, they are worth prioritizing, even when you get into a new relationship. Those people who have earned our trust and have stayed closest to us can give us feedback on our blind spots.

Because a relationship requires attention, it's going to pull some time and energy from other areas of your life. The people who know you the best can help you not trade so much that you lose sight of your other goals—and help you pick someone who is worth that time in the first place.

REWIND AND REFLECT

Our ultimate question when it comes to your Flame is whether they are a bright light in your life.

- Do they light the way to your ultimate goals?

- Do they keep that passion burning in you?

- Are they bringing good, positive things into your life?

- Is your life better with them in it, or worse?

Surround yourself with good people who will have your back and allow them to point out when you're slipping into unhealthy patterns. Lean on your SEAL Team. Give them permission to support you on your journey to your goals and to be a hardass with you when you need it. If a relationship is one of your goals, have them put the word out for you to help you find that person who aligns with you. Who better to be protective of you and value you than your closest, most trusted people? I have to hand it to my good friend Becca, the one who set me and Jason up on the blind date, knowing we would get along when

I wasn't so sure about what I needed at the time. Friends know you better than you think.

DO YOU TRUST YOURSELF?

This isn't easy. It's not like snapping your fingers and having someone appear, then cutting them off at the knees the second they mess up. Relationships are a dance. The more confidence you have in your intuition, how you want to be treated, and what you want from a relationship, the easier it will be to participate in that dance.

When I was in those bad relationships, my self-worth was horrible—but I didn't realize it at the time. In fact, everyone in the outside world saw me as a confident entrepreneur who could handle anything. But in relationships, my choices were terrible. Over and over, I'd let people into my life who had no business being there. Ultimately, I didn't think I was worthy of being treated any better than that.

If I learned any lesson from my bad relationships, it's that I hung on too long. The minute I ended them, it was like opening up a vacuum that brought good people into my life. When you spend so much energy and time on something negative that you just won't give up, there's no room for positive energy and the things that you do want. It stands in the way of everything else you're trying to accomplish.

If your only requirement is that the other person is good-looking and single, you're going to get what you get. You can start to narrow it down by looking for someone with a good job and ambition, who has a relationship with their parents, and who cares about the planet and giving back. Some pickiness will help to weed out a lot of the bad eggs who won't make you happy anyway.

When I finally sat down and made a list of what I wanted in a relationship, I was able to acknowledge my own wants and needs and to value them myself. And I stuck with it. If someone didn't measure up, I wouldn't waste my time with them. The universe has a funny way of not letting us move on to the best if we're still settling for the worst. Don't compromise, and don't hang on to someone who isn't holding you up.

This doesn't mean you have to spend every night at dinner with somebody new, like warp-speed interviews. You also don't have to spend all of your time with someone getting to know them. Practice slowly. Take baby steps toward that confidence. Start by saying no to a second date if the first one was bad. Check in with your intuition and whether your partner is in line with the rest of your life. Be deliberate. Be intentional. Make good choices, because you are capable, you're growing more and more confident, and you've always been worth it.

PAUSE AND PRACTICE

Time to make a list! I didn't realize how important that list was until I made it and started holding myself to it. Everything shifted. I spent ten years dating the wrong people, even though I knew what being with the right person felt like. My first husband had shown me the way. I *knew* better. But I had to intentionally remind myself of that. Now it's your turn. Make a list! Build out the ideal relationship—what do you want from a partner? What kind of person are they, and how do they treat you?

Once you have a list, share it with at least one member of your SEAL Team or with your champion. They want what's best for you, even in those low moments when you aren't sure of it yourself. You've got good things coming your way! Share some of the things on your list with #myshefactor.

CHAPTER SIX

FAITH

GET GROUNDED IN SOMETHING BIGGER THAN YOU

Faith is seeing light with your heart when all your eyes see is darkness.

—BARBARA JOHNSON

Not long ago, I went to a Counting Crows concert. I splurged on the whole VIP experience because they represented so much more than a band to me. You see, right before Bion died, the Counting Crows had released their album *August and Everything After*. To this day, I can turn it on and go right back to our last moments together and my long, wandering recovery afterward.

Losing Bion was like losing part of myself. After the crash and my rebound second marriage, I was back in pharmaceutical sales, a single mom, not really dreaming anymore. I put aside the business plans we'd made. I lost most of the $1 million settlement because I subconsciously didn't feel right hanging on to it for long. I'd been through a long custody battle, but that was over. There was nothing left to do. It was just me and my young daughter, Tori, and I didn't know at all who I was outside of that. The dust had settled from the five-year storm that had almost taken everything from me. Everyone had advice. No one really had answers. And I was struggling to find my way.

Finally, my brother brought me a mix CD.

Patrick has been obsessed with music since he was three, playing Beach Boys records obsessively. It's the best way he knew how to communicate with me, and the songs he picked were perfect. He included the Counting Crows, of course, and the music was cathartic. The songs seemed to be speaking right to me and let me brood a little bit when the world was pushing me to move on.

My brother brought more than a CD to me that day, though.

Shortly after the crash, which happened in mid-May of that year, I'd signed up to work with Canine Companions to raise a service dog. I wasn't supposed to hear anything back for six months, but by mid-summer they'd called. Someone had donated an eight-week-old golden retriever puppy, and they wanted to know if I could take her.

I still had our two big dogs—Mick and Winnie—who hadn't stopped needing to go on walks and to play, despite my horrible grief. They kept me getting up and out of bed every day. I decided I could do it, and Orie came home to me.

When you raise a Canine Companion, you have to take the dog with you everywhere. Literally everywhere—the grocery store, the mall, wherever—wearing their little companion vest. What do you think happens when you take a cute little puppy out into public wearing a cute little vest? People happen.

People swarm you. They want to know all about the puppy. They laugh. They smile. They make you feel good, whether or not you want to.

Orie brought me back out into the world, reengaging with people and being responsible for this little ball of fluff. And then, after about a year, she flunked out of the program. She wasn't meant for anybody else at all. She was meant for me.

My brother had watched this happen. He knew about the

Camp Bow Wow plan on the back of a napkin. And a few years later, he brought me a mix CD and the crazy idea to dig up Camp Bow Wow and make it happen. He brought me back to something bigger than myself.

FIND A CONNECTION AND HOLD ON TO IT

Faith isn't about religion necessarily, though for many people they are certainly connected. For me, religion wasn't a big player. We were raised as holiday churchgoers. I believed in God, even though I didn't understand too much about religion or faith at all. After the crash, I tried to understand what had happened from that perspective, but I didn't have a belief strong enough to say, "I get it." Once I connected with music and my dogs, I went inward to try to process it myself.

My first sparks of reconnection with faith came when I realized music and my dogs didn't exist on their own— they were connecting me to something else. They were leading me on to a different path, and I felt reassured that things were going to be okay.

Looking back, I can see that I was leaning on God. I wanted to know if he was there. If any of this was real. If my husband was with him, if he was okay.

When someone dies that suddenly and tragically, you just

want some sort of sign that they are okay. For months, I couldn't see anything like that. There was nothing. In those moments, you're forced to lean into the dark toward something bigger than yourself. You have to explore what you really believe about what happens after death. You're forced to confront all of those difficult questions.

I didn't have a Kumbaya feeling. I never thought "this was all supposed to happen." I kept questioning. But the more I'd question, the more I slowly started getting subtle reassurances. Prodding along.

Orie was one of those signs.

I hadn't planned to train a dog and certainly didn't have the capacity to, but Orie helped me start to move on. Tori was the next sign. I hadn't planned to have a baby either—remember my counselor told me the last thing I needed to do was get married or have a baby? When I found out that I was pregnant, I was terrified and an absolute mess. But God gave her to me so that I had something else to focus my love and energy toward.

Tori completely changed my life. She became the most important thing in the world to me and brought me back to myself. There really was more to accomplish in my life, more to be on this earth for, and all of these things that weren't "supposed" to happen were my reminders.

Now, I see those moments as part of a beautiful pattern that makes a bit more sense. Even all of the decisions that led to me losing the money—having so little left gave me the drive I needed in order to make Camp Bow Wow as successful as it was.

GET QUIET AND LISTEN

It's so much easier to connect to something bigger than yourself when you can get quiet. Our lives are difficult to settle down in normal life. While I was in the throes of grief and chaos, it was even harder to figure out what I needed to accomplish and why I was here.

Part of the reason that I found so much peace with Tori, music, and my dogs is that they brought me back to some stillness. I spent a lot of time walking the dogs, then when I moved in with Tori's dad, we lived in the mountains. With nature and music, I was able to get quiet and slow down. I reengaged in life in a different way, and that's what helped me connect to a higher power. I call it God, though you can refer to it as whatever force or power that you tap into. It brought me into something bigger than myself.

It was a purposeful kind of quiet, though—a stillness—and that makes a difference.

Pharmaceutical sales had been a strange industry to work

in. Back in the early '90s, healthcare looked so tumultuous that we'd get laid off from the company we were working for every year or so. Then, a month later, a different company would hire us. When the crash happened, I'd just been laid off. In fact, I had an interview scheduled for the next Monday. Needless to say, I didn't go. And then when I got the settlement, I felt like $1 million meant I could do whatever I wanted to, including not going back into pharmaceutical sales.

Even though I had this space to figure out what I wanted to do, it wasn't stillness. I didn't have Bion in my life, I didn't have a job to go to, and until I had Tori, I didn't have anyone in my life who was attached to me. It was almost paralyzing. There was so much pressure to figure out what I wanted to do, to figure out how I should move on and "get back to life."

Stillness is a feeling of being settled within yourself. It allows messages to come in. It helps you to find clarity. In my grief, I had to realize that it was a journey without a destination. Things weren't going to magically be okay one day. It was like losing a limb, and I had to learn to live life in a new way without that part of me.

Busyness wouldn't fill that space even though I did my darndest to make it so. I drove my family nuts trying to constantly create new things, see new things, and get involved in new things. I tried to fill up my time so that I didn't have any room to think about how sad I was. There was also an element of Carpe Diem, seizing the day, now that I'd realized how fragile life was. I thought I needed to get all kinds of things done without wasting any time doing things I loved or being around people I loved. I was almost frantic about it, with little tolerance for people who were relaxed and didn't have any expediency. Life could pull the rug out from under me at any moment. That's the lesson that lived in me from the crash, and from Steve walking away to marry someone else so abruptly.

There's a strange balance that I've found necessary since the crash. It is just as important to seize the day and make the most of your life as it is to be still, present, and quiet. When I got settled and learned to strike that balance, I found my relationship to something bigger again (what I call faith). That's when I found reassurances that we are all connected, and that my loved ones were fine. I found similar peace within grief later, after my grandparents passed away.

More recently, we suddenly lost my mother-in-law, who we all adored, to a tragic fast-moving bout of bone cancer. The day after she passed away, a baby bunny fell into our window well. I rescued it, and it sat quietly in my hands, just resting and staring at me while its little nose twitched away. In the weeks following (and every so often now), the kids and I would see baby bunnies all the time, and they would be quiet—peaceful, I would say—and gaze at us as long as we would engage them. It was reassuring to all of us; it felt like Jackie assuring us she was okay. Little affirmations and peace that there is something more out there, something after this life, show up in the quiet, underneath the chaos. To this day, there are certain songs that come on the radio, numbers I see, and sayings I'll hear that quietly remind me we're not alone without our loved ones.

REWIND AND REFLECT

The power of prayer, meditation, and quiet have been scientifically proven. That type of stillness can look like almost anything, as long as it quiets your mind and builds connection.

- Can you spend time meditating, thinking positively, or sending good thoughts out into the universe?

- Do you have a way to connect with your faith or belief in something bigger?

- Have you talked to your parents or grandparents about their beliefs?

Whatever form it takes, getting still works. Whatever you need to do to get quiet, do it. Pay close attention to the little things for the next few days. Butterflies, rainbows, songs that come on the radio. Just be still and see what you notice. Make your way back toward that higher power to connect, listen, and honor what the world is trying to tell you.

Humans aren't solitary animals. We all need to feel connected to something. The reason giving back makes you feel good is because you're honoring your role in your relationship to other humans. When you tap into that, your individual problems start to lessen. You're part of something much bigger than yourself.

If you get a handle on the foundation that we talked about in Part I—who you are, your passions, and even some connection to people around you—but miss this piece, you'll know it. There's a quiet confidence and a connection to your intuition that drives everything else that we're working on, and you can really only find that within some form of faith.

FAITH UNDER PRESSURE

Early on in my life, my faith was only topical. I'd go to church at Christmas, and I believed in God. But that was as far as it went. I was pretty bought into what people around me thought I should do and how I should live my life and what I should believe. The trauma that I experienced when Bion died ripped all of that down.

Grief leaves you angry and upset, trying to believe in something that might let you see your loved one again or connect you to them in some way. Even if you're an atheist and believe that we become part of the earth, a connection to the earth can bring you closer in that way. You're just left feeling desperate to connect, and that desperation forces you to examine what you really believe and then test it. Constantly test it.

Grief destroyed any preconceptions I had about faith, and it took a lot of time and work to get past my own insecurities and my sadness, enough to rebuild that connection. I had to not only decide what I actually believed, but I had to get confident enough in that belief that I could forge a path that embraced a commitment to living a different way. I'm a much more interesting and complete person having learned through these experiences. It feels like the process a rock takes to become a diamond—it's placed under tremendous pressure but comes out at the end much more beautiful.

It took a lot of pain and urgency to shake me hard enough to learn these lessons. Some of the lessons had to come to me several times over before I learned them. When you're going through those moments, it doesn't feel productive. It doesn't feel like anything beautiful can come from it. If I were twenty again, before so much of my life fell apart, I don't know how much I'd listen to someone telling me what to believe—but I would have loved someone giving me the confidence and tactics to figure it out on my own. That's what I want to leave you with in this chapter.

You get to figure it out. You get to decide.

You can get still and quiet and find your own faith. You can decide what this higher power is that you're connecting to, or if you even believe there is one, and how you want to communicate with it. Faith is so very personal and specific to each of us that no rulebook gets to say what that looks like. That genuine, personal connection can be the difference between isolation and connectedness. Only a faith of that sort will sustain you when life is at its hardest.

PAUSE AND PRACTICE

Faith is your intuitive connection that guides you toward your purpose. It's what motivates you to do good in this world, because of how we're all connected and affect each other. It's also how we can listen to the lessons that our life is teaching us. The lessons aren't always pleasant, but without stillness, we can't hear the reassurance to stay strong, believe, and keep going. For this exercise, I want you to find your stillness. If you already have a faith practice, reconnect with it. If you don't, I encourage you to explore different things until you find something that helps you connect.

Spend time praying or meditating. Spend time with people or animals, or simply spend time sitting in nature. When you find a practice that makes you feel connected to a higher power or people around you, begin to bring that into your everyday life. It's the balance between being driven and being still that helps us live life to the absolute fullest. If you'd like to connect with others about your faith journey, join the conversation with #myshefactor.

CHAPTER SEVEN

FREEDOM

STAY ENGAGED AND CONNECTED TO YOUR NEIGHBORS AND FELLOW CITIZENS

Freedom is never more than one generation away from extinction. We didn't pass it to our children in the bloodstream. It must be fought for, protected, and handed on for them to do the same.

—RONALD REAGAN

My little brother had my back. When he told me, "Let's get out those old plans for Camp Bow Wow. I want to see you find your passion again. How about we get it started?" I didn't jump on it right away. After several failed attempts at conventional businesses, I wasn't about to use the last

$83,000 of the settlement on an idea that everyone had told me was silly.

But the more I thought about it, the more I found that excitement again—and the more I felt like it was the right thing to do.

Since I was a single mom and needed the security, I kept my pharmaceutical job and started Camp Bow Wow "on the side." Tori and I would hang out at the parks south of downtown Denver around the location we'd chosen, and we'd hand out Milk-Bones with fliers for a free day of doggy day care. I would visit veterinarian offices while I was out in the field doing my pharmaceutical sales calls. I'd spend evenings dropping off fliers at local coffee shops and leaving messages for reporters, trying to drum up some press. My brother hired (and fired) staff and managed our furry friends in the play yards while juggling the phones and constant flow of walk-ins wanting to see what the heck doggy day care was. We found our rhythm, the dogs started coming, and Camp Bow Wow started to take off.

Then, the government found us.

Let me clarify. I don't mean that we were hiding. And I don't mean the government is inherently bad. (I'm part of it now, after all. More on that in a little bit.) The problem was that the interaction was completely arbitrary.

It was about six months into running the Camp when a zoning inspector from the city showed up, ready to fight.

"What do you think you're doing here?"

(Mind you, I'm surrounded by dogs playing and barking enough to drown out his gruff voice.)

"I'm...running a dog care business."

He said, "Well, the place isn't zoned correctly for that."

"Really? Because the commercial real estate guy told me it was when I signed the lease."

Apparently, no matter how true that was, he'd heard it before and wasn't convinced that it mattered. He laughed and told me never to trust brokers—and to come down to the city.

When I got there, I found our friend the zoning inspector behind stacks of massive books. Now, this was in the early 2000s, so it's not terribly surprising that everything was still on paper rather than computerized, but the process was so tedious it was almost funny. (Almost.)

There he was, flipping through page after page, trying to figure out what our business could be categorized as so that he could prove to me we were in the wrong kind of zoning. It wasn't a kennel, because we didn't keep them overnight. It was just dogs hanging out in a building.

He decided we were a warehouse that was "holding commodities"—the pets being the commodities—and suddenly became benevolent. "Young lady," he told me, "I don't want you to get hurt. I think your business idea is a bit nuts, babysitting dogs during the day? I'm worried about you and your safety. You shouldn't have more than fifteen dogs a day in there. That's the limit I'm putting on you."

Never mind the fact that I couldn't make any money with those limits, or that we'd been running just fine with fifty dogs at a time. Fifteen at most was the new rule. Signed and sealed. No committee hearings, no one to appeal to, no discussion.

We left that location and found one a couple of blocks away that was "zoned" for us—an old industrial building in a shady, do-what-you-want kind of neighborhood. Our doggies didn't mind, though, and we were able to grow until we were ready to open a second location and start the franchising process.

Holy cow. If we thought our friend with the stacks of books and feigned concern for my safety was frustrating, we had no idea what was coming. Franchising is the most regulated form of business on the planet.

The bigger Camp Bow Wow got, the more disgusted I became with how onerous it was to grow a business. By the time we reached thirty or forty franchise locations, the state of Colorado's Department of Agriculture—which is comprised of *appointed* positions rather than elected—brought in some purely bureaucratic rules for every doggy day care in the state. They told us we had to have one person for every fifteen dogs (there's that magic arbitrary number again) and that the dogs could never be left alone in the yard.

We were doing fine with one for every twenty-five dogs, and the *rest of the country* was allowed twenty-five dogs. But here in Colorado, with no justification at all, that cut our profitability by 20 percent per franchise location. As much as I tried to get the regulation changed, I couldn't get anyone's attention. No one seemed to understand or care that it was hurting an entire industry, all the way down to the people we had to charge more because of the increase in staffing.

To keep the dogs safe, my brother had come up with a brilliant idea to help us monitor the dogs and give customers (the human ones) a way to check in on their pups from anywhere in the world. A webcam in each play yard. We call them Camper Cams now, and millions watch them every day to see their pups playing at Camp. Our innovation was far more effective in keeping the dogs safe than the highly paid bureaucrats' method of slapping on a costly regulation. Regardless, we had to follow their rules, or they could shut us down.

My frustration was fully fueled. I became passionate that what we needed in our country was to help entrepreneurs and small business owners (not hurt them with a tidal wave of regulations) to create jobs, which improve the economy, give folks a hand up (not hand out), and fuel our economy. Little did I know just how far down the path to politics that would take me. No matter what your political beliefs are, or if you don't have any at all, stick with me—you might be surprised where this chapter takes you as well.

HOW I GOT EDUCATED, ENGAGED, AND EXCITED

Around 2012, a couple of years into Camp Bow Wow, two things happened. First, I went through a well-known community leaders' program in Colorado. My husband had just completed it and was tired of hearing me go on and on about how onerous government was to deal with in growing my business. The program is like civics on steroids. You learn all about the founding principles of the country, you re-read the Declaration, the Constitution, the Federalist papers...you really dig into the history of our country and why free markets are vital to the US of A.

The things America has brought to the planet are so cool. Global poverty has dropped dramatically, hunger has dropped to the lowest levels ever, and literacy has increased dramatically. It all hinges on the turning point that was America's founding. Free markets, individual rights, and property rights were all woven into this great experiment, and it changed the world. That whole course got me so excited and passionate about keeping the American dream alive, especially as I lived it out. I came from a very modest family, started a business, and wound up creating thousands of jobs and making a lot of kibble—er, money—not to mention giving a lot of it away to help pups around the world through our foundation, Bow Wow Buddies.

I wanted everyone to have that same opportunity to change their course and live the dream, but I saw it dying under government regulation, crony capitalism, and corrupt politicians. The difference between our potential and our reality made me sick to my stomach.

At the same time, I became more involved with the University of Colorado as I joined the business-school board, then was pushed up to the foundation board, which manages all of the endowments for the school. I wound up speaking all the time to groups throughout the campus, and before I knew it, someone suggested I should run for regent. The regents are like the board of directors for the University of Colorado system, which contributes over $12 billion to the state economy and is the fourth largest employer in Colorado.

We're one of only four states who elect the board of regents for their universities, and it's a position that showed up third on the ballot during the 2016 presidential election. The first time it was suggested to me, there was no way I had time to devote to that kind of a campaign. But by the time the election season came around, I'd sold Camp Bow Wow.

It seemed like the right time to run, especially since political advisors told me the race wouldn't be a big deal. They said no one pays attention to it, and they suggested I would easily win. I registered to run, announced my candidacy, and started traveling all over the state to talk to people about education and its tie to protecting the American dream.

Unfortunately, one of the top female politicians in the state decided to run for the same position, as a stepping stone to run for governor. Because she was running under the Democratic ticket—listed just under Hillary Clinton in a state that Hillary had in the bag—and she'd been Colorado's Speaker of the House for years, the race was no longer mine.

Advisors changed their tune. I wasn't going to win, but I should definitely stay in the race.

I'd been working my tail off for this race, and I don't do things to lose. If I was staying in the race, I was going to do all I could to win. That's when I recruited one of my best friends, Jill, to help lead my campaign, and it was us against the world. We quickly learned how to raise money and got clear on our messaging. I grew to love campaigning. I stuck to real issues and stayed away from all of the polarizing top-of-the-ticket issues that drove that election season. I showed people that I cared, because I genuinely did, whether it was through ads, speaking, or showing up at events. I came as me—as a happy warrior trying to make things better. And as the founder of Camp Bow Wow, I put a puppy in my ads, which didn't hurt.

And that's how I wound up a statewide elected official, running on a ticket with the party that lost to Hillary by 5 percent in our state. Our scrappy, ragtag, passionate campaign team had done what every political consultant and pollster said was not possible.

But that's my side of the story. What I'm even more excited about in this chapter is that you have a story coming that's all your own. It might not take you to a political office, and I certainly don't need you to be in the same party or even the same perspective as I am. But I want you to share that excitement and engagement with me because there's so much work to be done still.

HOW TO (REALLY) GET EDUCATED

All too often, from young people to the elderly, we pick our politics based on how popular they are in our circles. If we vote at all, it's based on what sounds good on the surface. We stick to the people who agree with us and don't dig any deeper to work toward actual solutions. We theorize about situations that we're not in and then stick to that perspective.

We're missing all of this in our education systems. You might have graduated from a high school that didn't have a debate club—one of the best places to learn how to see another perspective and hash out difficult topics from all angles. The odds are even better that you couldn't pass a citizenship test (only 19 percent of people under forty-five can).[3] I've tried to get the university to require a civics class that teaches people how to become an educated and engaged citizen, and the pushback is shocking. Simple

---

3   Allyson Escobar, "Most of us would fail the U.S. citizenship test, survey finds." NBC News, October 12, 2018. https://www.nbcnews.com/news/latino/most-us-would-fail-u-s-citizenship-test-survey-finds-n918961

things like learning about the electoral college, how many members of Congress there are, term limits, and local officials are controversial.

If we're not being taught how to engage in the system and effect change, we have to learn it ourselves. At no point in history has it been more important or accessible to learn about the issues and the potential solutions.

The best way to get informed is to listen. Read all kinds of opinions on a topic. Look specifically for opposing sides to an issue. Meet with people who have different opinions. Put yourself in situations where you'll be around people with very different views on life than your own. In other words, we can all educate each other.

A counselor that Jason and I see every once in a while gave us a book about two men, one Arabic and one Jewish, who were both teenagers when they lost their fathers to cultural and ideological war. As adults, they came to be best friends, and now they teach other people about how to deal with conflict. The book, *The Anatomy of Peace*, by The Arbinger Institute, is important, and so timely, because we're struggling to talk to each other in our country today. As I traveled across Colorado during my campaign (and still do), I was shocked by the difference in feedback from rural small-town Colorado and the big-city Denver metro area.

Depending on your environment, you likely can't speak up with a differing opinion if the whole class is on the other side. I see it from conservative and liberal kids alike. Even if you have well-reasoned arguments or points to consider, if you're going up against group-think, you're not likely to find a conversation and rational debate waiting for you. It's not even a matter of which side is right anymore—why can't we have a civil conversation that comes up with a solution that honors both perspectives?

In my experience, there are some things we can practice in order to get better at talking politics in today's charged environment.

Try not to start a conversation with the goal to prove someone is wrong or change their mind. Research shows us it's really hard to change our own minds, let alone someone else's.

Listen, listen, listen. Amaryllis Fox, a former clandestine service officer with the CIA, has some great advice. "Everybody believes they are the good guy. The only real way to disarm your enemy is to listen to them. If you hear them out, if you're brave enough to really listen to their story, you can see that more often than not, you might have made some of the same choices if you'd lived their life instead of yours."[4]

---

4   Celeste Headlee. "How to Talk About Politics Constructively." Retrieved on 12/28/2018: https://ideas.ted.com/how-to-talk-about-politics-constructively/.

I don't think she's saying you have to agree with their decisions, but by understanding their point of view, you can get some insight into why they believe what they do and bring some empathy to the discussion.

Finally, assume the person's point of view is coming from a place of care and love of our country and fellow citizens. We all want what is best; we just have different ideas on how to solve the problems. If we can both bring our best ideas to the discussion, perhaps we can find compromise and keep our friendships.

REWIND AND REFLECT

Can you stretch yourself to think about politics in a new way?

Try asking yourself some of these questions the next time you feel challenged about an issue to help get past partisan thinking and into reality.

- Why do they believe what they do?

- What solution do they think is best and why?

- Where can you find common ground, even in the smallest way?

Then, ask the other person some probing questions as well, like *how would that work, can you explain what you mean, how might that impact…?* etc.

As an example, if you care about gender equality, research all of the perspectives and solutions, beyond the sound bites and op-eds. Talk to employers about it. Listen to employee stories. Find some empathy for people on all sides of the issue, from what it is to actually run businesses to career pathways for employees.

If you care about immigration, or the second amendment, or climate change—engage all sides of the issue. Whatever you're interested in, learn as much as you possibly can, then use your critical-thinking skills to make your mind up about it.

That kind of systematic civil debate and collaborative discussion—free thinking—built this country. That's how you solve the hardest problems in society. You debate like crazy, picking ideas apart until you've found the best and brightest of all sides. You don't get to those conclusions with outrage machines and mob mentality. Without free thinking and open debate, we're being torn apart.

WHY GET ENGAGED

One of the founding principles that we often misunderstand is the right to pursue happiness. Our constitution does not guarantee us any sort of happiness—only the ability to pursue it. The responsibility to take advantage of that right falls on our shoulders. It's not up to the government to make you happy, but even deeper than that, it's not up to your parents or your boss or your peers either.

Humans work best when we're incentivized to work hard, get that feeling of fulfillment, and find success. You've picked up this book because you're powerful and fierce, and you want to create something amazing in your life. You have the motivation to pursue happiness. An outflow of that motivation is the responsibility to protect that freedom for future generations.

You don't have to go out and run in a hotly contested statewide race, though plenty of young women are doing just that. Voting is a good start, as long as you're bringing that self-education factor in and learning the issues inside and out. Don't just vote down ballot or learn only about one side—hang out with people on the other side as well. Learn about the process that led to those issues, about our country, about why we were founded in certain ways, about why we operate the way that we do. Even though you may have covered it in civics back in high school, read the Declaration of Independence and the Constitution again. Try the Federalist papers if you dare.

You can show up at town halls, debates, and rallies. Support the candidates you believe in. Canvas and help educate others. Work on a campaign or a ballot initiative. In Colorado, we have the ability to change our constitution through ballot initiatives, so every election, there are tons of issues on the table. The whole state can change completely with one successful ballot initiative, so those are highly effective to work on.

"Be the change you want to see" absolutely applies to politics, government, and society. Be willing to get involved and model what your ideals should look like. We're all responsible for ourselves and our own actions. We all have a pathway to effect change, in some way. It's hard work, but the truth is that if you're not actively engaged in the process, you're standing in its way.

It's hard work to protect this grand experiment called America and the vision it was built with. The Founding Fathers knew it wasn't going to be easy to keep our republic alive and well and suggested that if we didn't keep an educated citizenry, it would die. Just like every other area of focus, you don't have to go all in here—we're all balancing and trading our time. But neither can you completely neglect it, as it affects every area of our lives. Take baby steps. Maybe that's researching one issue or simply asking your employer if they have a committee on an issue you're concerned about. You might find that you're ready to lead the political charge or that you want to work on the private side of an issue you care about.

Wherever you go from here, just be brave and dip your toe in! Politics has become a brutal topic and a difficult space to engage. But you're growing in your confidence and authenticity, in choosing things to be passionate about, in surrounding yourself with supportive people, and in learning to approach conflict in meaningful ways. You're connecting with something beyond just yourself. That makes you exactly the kind of change we need in this world, and we're all going to be better for it.

PAUSE AND PRACTICE

You're part of this great American experiment, and you get to direct its future. Nothing we do is without consequence, so don't sell yourself short on the impact that small actions can have. Start with something small but meaningful. Work on educating yourself thoroughly on one issue or get engaged in a way you haven't yet. Can you take one issue that's important to you and explore both sides of it? Or, if you're already educated on a topic, can you take one step toward action on it? Join the conversation and encourage your fellow SheFactor citizens with #myshefactor.

CHAPTER EIGHT

FAVOR

THE ART OF THE COMEBACK
IS TO GIVE BACK

A grateful heart is a beginning of greatness. It is an expression of humility. It is a foundation for the development of such virtues as prayer, faith, courage, contentment, happiness, love, and well-being.

—JAMES E. FAUST

In 2009, my little Hollie was born. At one of our visits a few years later to our pediatrician, Dr. Bucknam (aka Dr. Bob) asked about Tori. He'd been our pediatrician for years, and by that point, Tori was in high school. The truth was, Tori had been struggling. The whole school was dealing with some real challenges, including drugs and alcohol, internet bullying, and anxiety about what had just happened at Sandy Hook Elementary School.

"Oh, she's okay, I guess," I told him. "Honestly, high school has been a real struggle. She and her friends all seem to be going through some tough stuff. Times are different now, and I'm not quite sure what else I can do to support her."

"Here's my advice," he said. "When I see that kids are struggling, I tell parents to get them focused on volunteering or helping other people. When kids realize that they're part of something bigger, giving back usually gets them feeling better about themselves, feeling more connected to their community, and seeing the importance of their role on this planet. That usually does the trick."

His thoughts were welcome, as always, and I sat with that idea for a while. I looked back on the areas of my life where I'd come back from something big. I thought about helping to raise Orie after the plane crash and how that brought me back into the world. I thought about Tori herself and what it meant to me to focus on caring for her and realizing the role I had to play in her life and in the world. I thought about starting Camp Bow Wow and taking care of my employees and our franchisees—how much work I'd done to help them live out their own dreams.

He was exactly right. In every area of my life where I had

to come back from a really hard time, I would reengage in life by focusing my energy outward on something or someone else. It's why we are so fulfilled by being the change we want to see in our workplaces and government. When you give someone an opportunity to be part of something bigger or to be a productive human being, it's so much better than just getting a check. Studies even show that the best welfare program is to get someone a job where they feel accepted and cared for, where they feel valued. That sense of worth and connection, more than anything, changes things for people.

This is why we focus so much on finding your passion, discovering your purpose, and living your own life. Committing to living a life of purpose is what leads to that fulfillment that we're all looking for. If you were blessed enough to be born with the ability to pursue that purpose—with freedoms, family, support, and the ability to live your own life in the way that you want—how are you going to honor those gifts?

Now more than ever, your generation senses the urgency to protect and maximize this amazing life we have access to. Things are shifting so rapidly that if we don't fight for it, we will surely lose it. The only way we can do that is to break down the molds—the ideas we have about what it means to have faith, to protect our freedoms, and to share the favor we've been given with other people. If we can get to something more authentic and true, we can build it back up together. It takes bravery, vulnerability, and hard work, but it's how we stay connected to each other and the world around us.

> ## MOMS FIGHT BACK
>
> My gifts are not in operational work, running projects, or doing research, but I've been at the helm of two different foundations now. Most recently, I formed Moms Fight Back, which was a response to an experience my daughter had with assault and the aftermath that followed. A friend of mine was working on an effort called Girls Fight Back, and when she saw the work I was doing to support my daughter, encouraged me to work with other moms who wanted to defend, support, and protect their kids.
>
> Moms Fight Back is now part of the Fight Back Foundation. We're a social incubator, and this year we held a contest. We asked for big ideas about how to solve kids' social issues in our state. The twelve finalists had great ideas for non-profits, products, or services to help kids with drugs and alcohol, internet safety, bullying, teen suicide—and moms, too, addressing parental leave and being a new mom. The winners received a grant and a year of mentoring. I'm able to offer a much higher value to these budding entrepreneurs—who are all following their passions—than if I'd tried to run each of those efforts on my own. We all win when we work together to effect change.

GENUINE GENEROSITY

We're often taught to approach favor and service as another box to check off in a successful life. In the same way that we look at potential careers based on their income potential rather than a personal match, we often look at volunteering as an obligation that we have to fulfill. Because of that, we're also undersold on how valuable it is.

Once you recognize that you're part of something bigger and connected to other human beings and the planet, it's almost immoral to not share yourself, your energy, and your resources with other people. Without helping other people up, you're pushing yourself down.

If you're supporting causes you believe in and watching the people you're helping become happier, better members of society, it fills your own soul. If we really are part of something bigger, then ignoring our connection to each other is like only taking care of one room in the house. There's this odd balance between genuinely wanting to help others *and* knowing that it's going to help you as well.

Like everything else in your life, *favor* can't come from obligation or someone else's expectations. You have to get there on your own. You won't do any good for yourself or others by just adding this to your checklist. Giving back once a week or volunteering for the sake of it is an empty gesture.

Really sharing favor, in a way that builds others up as well as yourself, is intuitive. It comes from a true connection to an issue, person, or cause. If you find the right way to give, you'll feel compelled to do it from that place of passion that's driving everything else in your life. I'll never tell you to just give for the sake of giving. Take time to find the right thing to give your energy and passion to so that you are getting as much fulfillment out of the work as the people you are helping are getting from you.

I care about protecting the American dream of opportunity, improving our education system to make sure every child has the best shot at success, and helping young women launch their careers and lives (and pups, too, of course!). My focus on favor usually exists in those spaces. But we all care about different things. When you line your favor up with your passion, you're going to feel great about giving your energy and time back to that cause rather than feeling drained or taken advantage of. At this point, I don't make money on most of what I'm doing. I'm in a phase of life where service can be my priority, and it's incredibly fulfilling and energizing.

There's also going to be seasons where giving looks different to you for a while. When I was building Camp Bow Wow, we had our foundation, but my real focus was on building the business. Later, when I had Hollie and then the twins, I had to shift my focus inward again. Giving back to the world for me now includes raising good kids. Inward care, taking care of ourselves and our families, is an important form of favor that takes up a lot of energy in certain phases of life.

TIME, TREASURE, AND TALENT

Favor is a tangible expression of the connection you build in faith and the responsibility that you have to your neighbors, thanks to freedom. I like to think of favor as sharing of your time, treasure, and talent. Treasure is what we usually think about when we give favor, which is our next chapter, but money isn't the only way to share with others. For example, if you have a background in marine biology, you might volunteer on the coast with people helping to save whales, giving of your talents. Or you might volunteer in a soup kitchen or mentor kids who are learning to read, giving of your time.

Charitable giving was always an important part of the culture at Camp Bow Wow, but in 2007, we found where we really fit. Some of us on the corporate team took a ten-day trip to help animal welfare workers in Greece. When we got there, our hearts broke. The workers didn't have many resources available, and we found street dogs who'd been tied up in a lot—not just for a little while, but for several *years*. People would drop food and water off, but they couldn't leave the lots they were tied to.

We couldn't leave them there, and after some shifty work

getting twenty-six dogs on an international flight, we brought them home with us. Those "Greekies" became the starting point for the Bow Wow Buddies Foundation, which went on to foster dogs at every Camp Bow Wow, adopt out over ten thousand dogs, and raise $1 million for canine cancer research.

There's no right or wrong way to share with others. The important thing is to pay attention to both your own strengths and passions and to the opportunities around you. Don't just wait until your budget can justify giving financially. If you aren't sure where to look, this is a good time to check in with your champion or SEAL Team. Get some perspective on the way that things you are about and are good at can translate into opportunities.

REWIND AND REFLECT

Favor is something that you share with others outside of your job or things that monetarily benefit you, but ultimately is going to give back to you as well. It does far more for the person who is giving than for the recipient and is often the thing missing from our lives. If you're struggling to think about how to give more of yourself to others, reframe it. Ask yourself these questions:

- What social issues am I most passionate about fixing?

- What charities are my friends or family involved with that interest me?

- What am I able to give of my time, talent, and treasure?

Once you know the type of issue you'd like to help with, start asking around. Your friends and family might already be involved in organizations that can get your wheels turning. Do some research—you can use Guide-Star or Charity Navigator, which are online databases of charities ranked based on their reputation. You never know what kind of good is happening around you until you start looking with purpose.

I wound up giving a TED talk about my experience with hitting rock bottom and coming back again, and I called it "The Art of the Comeback." I wouldn't have been able to come all the way back from my struggles without also sharing that favor with others.

It was the common thread in all of my life stories and all the adversity. To come back, I gave back. When the plane crashed, caring for Mick and Winnie got me out of bed every day, then caring for Tori brought me back to life. Helping franchisees see their dreams come true made me smile, and seeing the foundation give thousands of dogs a home made the comeback all the sweeter.

Giving to others makes a deposit into your soul. All of those resources are finite, and we have to decide how to parse them out. When you budget your time, talent, energy, and finances for your soul first, you can better budget for the rest of your life.

We make investments assuming that we'll get something back on them. But authentic giving can't really come with expectations, even though we know that it'll be good for our souls as well. The best return on investing in favor happens when we're driven by passion and authenticity rather than selfishness, expectations, and obligation. The less you expect for yourself going in, the more pleasantly surprised you'll be by the outcome for you and the people you are serving.

PAUSE AND PRACTICE

If you still have your Mind Map from chapter 2, discovering your passions, break it back out for this exercise. Your passion is about far more than the way you can best give time, talent, and energy to a career—it's like a compass for your whole life. Whatever you discovered about how your life is best spent can be layered into *favor* as well.

What does that map tell you about the issues you care about? Where are you energized, and what drives you to get out of bed in the morning? Note where your areas of interest connect with your time, talents, or treasure. The sweet spot will be using your passions and highest energy points, combined with time spent giving back to others so you can connect to humanity on a higher level. Brainstorm some out-of-the-box ways to give back with #myshefactor.

CHAPTER NINE

FINANCES

A GOOD RELATIONSHIP WITH MONEY LETS YOU AFFORD THE LIFE YOU WANT

Money isn't the most important thing in life, but it's reasonably close to oxygen on the "gotta have it" scale.

—ZIG ZIGLAR

Camp Bow Wow grew to be a $100 million brand, and the investments from the sale allow me to live a life of passion and service today. But before any of that, I was a broke recent college graduate, a young newlywed, a "millionaire," and then broke again—all within less than a decade.

When Bion died, we had been living paycheck to paycheck.

I was twenty-seven and working in pharmaceutical sales, and he was finishing up his last year of college, about to have his twenty-fifth birthday. We'd just bought a house, had a ton of student loan debt, and came from families that struggled financially. We were pretty broke.

Together, we'd always joked about winning a million bucks through the lottery. He played religiously—mapping out numbers and whiteboarding it to "scientifically" figure it out. Having that money from the plane crash in my account seemed like such a cruel joke.

I now know that I wasn't even close to alone. Think about the way people react to winning the lottery. About 70 percent of lottery winners wind up going bankrupt within just a few years.[5] Now add grief to the equation and think about how difficult that windfall would feel. Money and spending are so emotionally connected that it becomes a subconscious way to not deal with the circumstances surrounding that windfall. You almost get rid of it out of guilt. It sounds ridiculous, but it's absolutely true. I didn't realize that at the time, either, so I fell right in line with the statistics.

Ultimately, I learned to create a better relationship with

---

5   Paul Golden. "Research Statistics on Financial Windfalls and Bankruptcy." Retrieved on 12/28/2018: https://www.nefe.org/Press-Room/News/Research-Statistic-on-Financial-Windfalls-and-Bankruptcy.

money, but I had to learn a lot of hard lessons about myself, other people, and money motives to get there.

CURB EMOTIONAL SPENDING

It all happened very quickly. We'd just purchased a $250,000 life insurance policy for each of us, and there was a seventy-five-day waiting period. The crash happened on the seventy-fifth day, so his policy helped me to get my feet under myself financially. Then, I got a call from the pilot's insurance company.

I hadn't thought at all about their insurance or anything that I might have been owed. The plane was an old '43 Stearman, like Snoopy's Red Baron plane, that was owned by a good friend of ours. They were family friends, and I never would have thought to sue or hold them responsible. When all was said and done, and it came out to $1 million, I was told I could take a breather and heal for a while. Instead, I just felt gross.

What took me forever to learn is that we use money to pacify ourselves when we don't feel good. It's like emotional eating. Spending is tied so closely to how we're feeling in the moment that it's easy to lose track of what's happening. It becomes more about trying to fill a need inside of us in the moment than using that money or food as tools for our wellness or future.

Having really clear goals about what you want your financial future to look like in a year, three years, five years, and ten years helps to change that dynamic. When you know where you're going, you can set boundaries about what you spend your money on and how you carve out your paychecks. You can also celebrate the small wins along the way that add up to big dollars over the long run!

When I was spending the settlement money, I didn't have any kind of clear target. Everyone told me I *should* buy this or that stock and I *should* try sensible investments and I *should* be generous with people, but I didn't know where I wanted to go or what I wanted to do. By the time Camp Bow Wow came up for consideration, and most of the money was gone, the tone changed. Suddenly, everyone who'd advocated spending started telling me, "Are you kidding me? How could you think of wasting more of that money—and on dog day care? Keep your day job!"

The difference was that I had a clear goal. I was down to the last bit of money, and I wanted to redeem myself, in a way. Camp Bow Wow had been a dream that Bion and I shared, and I only wanted to make up for the money that I'd lost. My smaller initial attempts at businesses failed, but when I sold Camp Bow Wow, the amount of money I made wound up being exactly the amount I'd have made if that settlement had been invested properly in the first place. I felt like I'd finally honored Bion's memory. The big difference was that I focused on a more positive emotion (hope and determination rather than guilt) and had a clear goal that I could stay committed to.

In order to effectively spend money today, you have to have a plan for your future and a lot of discipline. Having a vision of what you want and where you are going will stop you from focusing on the smaller emotional returns in that moment. A cute sweater now or a condo down the road?

FINANCE YOUR BEST LIFE

Back then, when I got the settlement, the assumption was that $1 million was enough to live on forever. Of course, that was ridiculous. The myths persist even today, with so-called budget gurus and advisors calling for unrealistic budget allotments, like only living on 50 percent of your income. They make it sound so simple to just download data from your bank account, easily see what's happening, and then fix it in a snap.

The truth is, budgets and spending are terribly hard.

It's true that you have to keep tabs on your finances or, little by little, it all goes away. The fall after the crash, I moved up to El Jebel, a small town outside of Aspen, to take time off with my dogs, which is where I started hanging out with my old friend, Tori's dad, and that chain of events was set into motion. I loaned money to family and friends, who came out of the woodwork looking for help and investments. I took my family on a cruise over Christmas. I'd tried to start a baby-bedding catalog company right after I had Tori, but having customers get mad at me about their orders was not the fulfilling business I had in mind, so I lost my passion for it quickly. It lasted a year and a half and cost me about $150,000.

From the get-go, I worked with a financial planner who was highly recommended, trying to maximize the settlement and invest it well—then realized later that he put most of it into variable annuity insurance policies that earned him big commissions and cost me in huge penalties, taxes, and limited access to the money.

Meanwhile, I was just lost.

Within a few years, I was down to very little money and had become a single mom embedded in a nasty custody battle with my ex-in-laws as they fought to enable and protect their abusive son. Over the next five years, I spent half a million dollars trying to protect my daughter from his addictions. I could see the money going away quickly and knew that I'd made poor decisions to make that happen.

Because I wanted to keep other people from going through

these same patterns, I decided to get my Certified Financial Planner designation and start The Maginot Group.

The Maginot Line is where France held off Germany's invasions for a while during World War II. My thought was that we could set up a defense around my client's money, especially those who received sudden wealth through insurance, the lottery, or any other type of windfall. I'd help them set up a team of people to protect the money and help them figure out how to handle it—all while I'd just blown most of my million. I felt like if I charged them I was taking advantage of them just like everyone else. While I held back on my investment into that company and kept it to more of a hobby, it still wound up being a loss.

The money dwindled away in small ways too. I'd pay for lunches, dinners, concert tickets for friends and family, because they had been such a big help throughout my painful ordeal. There's that guilt again.

If you don't keep track of where your money is going, you're just not going to meet your goals. And if you aren't emotionally strong and healthy around your money, you'll sabotage those goals. You won't get that nicer car or the house you want or the mission trip you hope to take.

Most of America lives paycheck to paycheck, figuring it

out as they go. In this game, we're going for the gusto. SheFactor is all about setting goals and reaching them, and if some of your goals are financial, you're going to have to do the hard things necessary to reach them.

REWIND AND REFLECT

Money gives us things like freedom to travel, a way to give back, a great house to live in, fun and meaningful experiences, and a sense of security. Ask yourself:

- What do you want money to do for you?

- What experiences do you want in life?

- What do you want your life to look like in a year? Three years? Five years? Ten?

- What do you want your relationship with money to look and feel like?

SET CLEAR BOUNDARIES

Money can be devastating to relationships. For some reason, many people feel entitled to other folks' money. Though settlements are riddled with guilt, it's easy to feel guilty in any situation where you have more than someone else does. People ask because they feel entitled, and you give because you feel guilty. That's a horrible dynamic.

Money is hard on relationships. Don't get me wrong. It can be helpful to people, for sure. Some of the people I helped with settlement money really did get out of a tight situation, but it's much better for the relationship when you have healthy boundaries and then can sometimes surprise someone with a gift or effect larger change by funding a foundation. The only way to reach that point is to be wise with your money early on.

Again, we're always making trades. You have to ask yourself whether paying for that bill for your boyfriend is worth setting your goals back *and* what it will cost in the relationship. From early relationships to later steps like moving in together and getting married, money carries so much weight. The way you mix it, the rights you have to it, and the boundaries surrounding it are complicated topics. We've already talked about how finances carry a lot of emotional weight, and that makes these conversations even harder. It requires a lot of frank, authentic, brave discussions.

It's much easier in the short term to just stay quiet and make assumptions when money's involved. Money problems can start to slip in quietly, in all sorts of ways. If you buy one hundred dollars' worth of groceries and he doesn't offer to chip in, that's tension. If you don't speak up, that tension will start to build. Just being open in that moment and asking for what you need—holding your boundaries and being clear in communication—can cut through the tension before it turns into something bigger.

I get it. It's hard, but it's crucial to have those tough conversations early on.

That confidence and clarity needs to show up in every area of our lives. You can absolutely stand up for yourself without being bitchy. You're the best person to advocate for yourself, whether it's in a relationship with a partner or a working relationship with a boss.

Know your worth. Know your goals. Employers respect that quality in a person, and any partner or friend who is worth the relationship will honor it as well. When someone would come to me at Camp Bow Wow saying, "Here's the value I bring to the company, and here's the raise I think I deserve," I was so proud of them for speaking up. Even when we couldn't give them what they asked for, we'd work toward it. But if no one brought it to my attention, I would just assume they were happy.

Critical conversation is an incredibly important skill to develop. Know what a successful outcome looks like, listen carefully for those motivations and underlying personality types, and factor that in. When you see red flags that tell you this isn't working and your boundaries are being tested, take those steps back to refocus on yourself, your passion, and your goals.

DIFFICULT LESSONS LEARNED

Your generation of young women has a drive to be independent and secure. You don't want to rely on family or a significant other, and that's admirable. But there also seems to be a roadblock when it comes to knowing how to do that. Good financial health hasn't been modeled well for most of us. If you start with the lessons and tools from this chapter, then bring what you know about yourself, your goals, and your personal accountability into it as well, you'll have a much better financial start than your peers or your parents' generation ever did.

Selling Camp Bow Wow came with a windfall that was much larger than the settlement, but I didn't spend time spinning my wheels. I didn't blow the cash. I didn't lose relationships. What I'd learned earlier in life helped me to thrive.

I was much more aware of how quickly the money could go, which made me much more protective of my decisions around that money. I did a lot of prep work when I picked a money manager—I checked references and researched who my team might be. I set specific goals about what success would look like if I managed it correctly.

There's no comparison between the way people spend large amounts of money that they've earned and money that has been given to them. The stats reflect this in a much more positive way. I think it's because you have time to get your sea legs. You put the work into the money, and you're proud of having it. Settlements and windfalls almost feel tainted, and you subconsciously want to get rid of them as quickly as possible.

Because I knew exactly what my passions were, I was able to move right into working on the Fight Back Foundation and joining some great nonprofit boards. About a year later, I started my run for elected office. I still took time to play and experiment, but because I knew who I was and where I was going, there was a peace to it. I wasn't frantically grasping for something that might stick, and I wasn't leaning on everyone else to tell me what to do.

SIMPLE, PRACTICAL APPLICATION

One of the most brutal lessons we all learn about money is that it's so much harder to earn it than it is to spend it. The clearest picture of this truth shows up when money comes unexpectedly—from a tragic windfall or a bonus at work or a gift from someone. Now, often we don't think much of these moments, because the money wasn't "earned" and we aren't really any worse off when it's gone. But look closer, and you'll learn more about how you spend money in the day-to-day as well.

It's hard to separate that money from the event that

brought it to you and the emotions tied to it. That little thrill of extra income—maybe from a bonus or a gift—makes spending easy. In the moment, it feels good to go shopping or for a night out, just like eating our feelings. *Stress calories don't count, right?* When we aren't feeling great and turn to carbs and sweets, those foods are filling a need inside of us more than they're filling our stomachs—and there's always a price to pay.

We spend money the same way. When we're wrapped up in emotional lows and highs, we often bring spending into the picture. Not only with windfalls but, unfortunately, with our typical budgets as well. That's where we really get into trouble.

Just like watching what we eat—even when we're stressed—we have to bring some awareness into the way we spend money. Check yourself every time you feel like spending money—if you're saving up to buy a condo, do you really need to lose forty dollars to a new sweater? Is it worth the extra time it will take to get you to that goal? Keep some notes on your phone about how you are feeling emotionally when you splurge. You may see some patterns that you can nip in the bud.

We don't have to let budgets and goals create unnecessary pressure either. Some of the ideas out there about how a budget should work are ridiculous and just make things harder. The simpler you keep it, the more likely you are to succeed. Even now, I have my ideal monthly budget that I compare against my actual spending. I figure up how much money I have to spend for the year, then break it down per month. There are annual expenses and monthly expenses, and when it's all broken down, I can track it every month.

The key is to keep doing the work to track how much you're spending. If you want to spend $1,000 a month and you wind up spending $1,500, can you cut back on going out to dinner next month to change that total? Long-term goals can come with short-term rewards as well. If you're saving for a house, 80 percent can go toward the house while 20 percent goes toward that new leather jacket. By checking in with yourself in simple ways, you can hold yourself accountable to your goals.

I'm not saying it's easy. In fact, it's terribly difficult. Not only do we have to make ourselves brave enough to do it, but it's a lot of work too. You can't just download your bank account like "they" tell you to do. There are categories and details that you're going to have to work out. Programs like Mint or Quicken help to make it a little bit easier, helping you set a budget and watch for trends. But at the end of the day, it's on you. You've got to commit to holding yourself accountable—yep, there's that personal responsibility thing again.

No one is going to make you do this. If you regularly spend what you'd planned to save, that's totally fine by everyone else's standards. But you're not going to make your goals. You're not going to buy a house or a better car or move beyond the paycheck-to-paycheck life that so much of America lives.

Don't trade your life away in order to keep up with your friends, keep up with appearances, or meet external expectations. Money is a tool that you can use to create the life you're dreaming of—be intentional with it, before it gets out of hand and starts to control you.

PAUSE AND PRACTICE

Don't worry. I'm not going to ask you to do a complete budget overhaul right now. And I won't tell you some out-of-touch numbers that your budget "should" fit into. Instead, I just want you to start practicing on some small things. If you already know what your daily budget is, then keep an eye on it. Compare what you're spending against what you've budgeted. Is your plan realistic? Do you need to make a better plan to stay on track?

Whether or not you have a budget, keep an eye on your spending for a week. Not only how much you spend, but also what it feels like. What emotions are you experiencing when you swipe that card? How do you feel afterward? What does it feel like if you put some money away to save? Keep notes in your journal for a week. Start to clue into the emotions that drive your spending, so that when you start to set goals, you know more about yourself and what you'll need to do to meet them. Then join us to practice talking about money with other SheFactor folks at #myshefactor.

CHAPTER TEN

FASHION

SHOW PEOPLE WHO YOU ARE
AND WHERE YOU'RE GOING

I like my money right where I can see it: in my closet.

—CARRIE BRADSHAW, *SEX AND THE CITY*

My favorite jobs have always included strategy and tactics related to marketing and building a brand. I love the creative component and the big ideas. In the beginning at Camp Bow Wow, I was the one responsible for creating the brand and bringing customers (furry and human) in the door, while my brother ran the day to day. During my campaign, I was able to be hands-on with the ads and messaging. If I go all the way back to childhood, it's what I've wanted to do since my aunt and uncle let me spend time with them at their creative agency.

It's probably not a surprise that my first thoughts about fashion are connected to branding, billboards, and a creative canvas.

When I create or grow a brand, the first thing I try to figure out is the message I'm trying to convey. Then I want to know who I want to hear that message and how I can connect with them in an effective, powerful way. And then my last consideration is how much money I need to make all of that happen.

In the last couple of years, I noticed that my friend and coach, who helped me back in chapter 2, was looking really great. Turns out, she'd worked with a stylist, Keri, who came to her home and helped her refocus her entire wardrobe. It was an expensive, time-consuming process, she warned me, but completely worth it.

She said that Keri would come throw out any clothes that didn't jive with the image I wanted to present to the world. She would take the time to learn anything and everything she could about me, my life, and how she could dress me for success. Then, without me, she would go shopping. I would meet her at her studio when she was done to discover my new, condensed, more focused wardrobe.

Knowing what I know about branding, and since my work is in the public eye, it made sense to me that my closet full of throwback outfits to the eighties might not be fresh, so I did it. Everything went exactly as my coach had said it would, except for one piece: my reaction. Not to what she bought for me—those clothes were amazing. Every single piece hit the mark in an incredible way. Keri knows exactly what to get, what critical pieces to include, and how to convey exactly the look you're going for.

What I didn't expect was how emotionally draining it would be to have her get rid of my old clothes.

The day after she was at my house, I felt like I'd been hit with a truck. She donated my favorite sweaters, my Van Halen T-shirt, and everything I'd been hanging on to "just because." I had no idea how emotionally attached I'd been to those pieces! I don't miss them now, but in the moment, it was horrifying.

In the same way that we spend and eat our feelings, clothes are closely tied to emotions and nostalgia. If you think about it, you probably emotionally spend money on clothes or change into a certain outfit just as when you grab comfort food. Fashion is powerful, both inside and out, and can reflect what we want to achieve as well as what we're trying to grow out of. Getting intentional about what you wear can ripple out and affect the way you feel about every other aspect of your life, not unlike a well-placed marketing campaign or a beautifully rendered canvas.

CHASING VERSUS BEING

Typically, we think of fashion as its own moving target. We *chase* trends, *keep up with* looks, and are always looking ahead to know what the next season will offer. Some of us give up the chase and let the world of fashion pass us by altogether. I was definitely the former, though a good friend of mine was the latter.

Not just good friends but one of my best friends, we've known each other since we were twelve. She has always dressed with one thing in mind: *comfort*. She'd always wear big sweaters or baggy jeans and high-top Reeboks, even as recently as a few years ago. Every birthday (after I could afford it), I'd get her a cute outfit. I even took her shopping to try to get her to try new clothes, which was a blast. But when it came down to it, my bestie had her priorities. "I'm fine," she'd tell me. "I'm comfortable!"

I even kiddingly, or not, submitted her (and told her I was doing it) to the old TV show *What Not to Wear*! She thought that was hilarious but refused to go on if she was selected.

At some point, though, I noticed a shift. It was right around the time that she started to sell Lia Sophia jewelry as a side hustle. One piece at a time, she shifted her clothing choices to coordinate with the goals she was aligning with. It was so fun to watch this dramatic change start to unfold more and more. The more encouragement she got, the more polished she'd get, until it steamrolled into a new style that was still her and still comfortable, but focused on who she was becoming.

I was completely the opposite. I chased trends like nobody's business, and my fashion reflected it; I dressed for what I wanted to blend in with rather than what I was. Since I grew up through the '80s, you can imagine how that played out.

In my heavy metal phase (yes, that happened, and still kind of does), my friends and I would go to concerts all the time. Of course, I did everything I could to fit in. I did the ripped jeans and the high-five hair, with black leather everywhere I could get it.

We're not even going to talk about the Madonna phase before that.

When I went to SMU my first year of college, I was suddenly surrounded by preppy oil-money kids in Dallas. They all drove BMWs, wore Rolex watches, and dressed impeccably. I showed up driving a '66 Mustang in my quasi-heavy metal gear, and I stuck out like a sore thumb. My roommate, Melanie, was a gorgeous homecoming queen, dance team, small-town Texas kind of girl. She kicked me into gear and helped me get my act together as a Dallas/Highland Park SMU girl.

When I later transferred to Boulder, it was all about Sorel boots and big ol' sorority letter sweatshirts to get through the snowy walks to class.

I did okay keeping up in each of these spaces, until I moved to San Diego right after college. More specifically, I moved to La Jolla, making $1,100 a month. This is when I was working at an ad agency and splitting an apartment with my friend, but we decided to hang out with yacht club folks. It was time to step up my game, which takes a massive budget.

I use "budget" loosely, because we were eating happy hour food for dinner and hoping someone would buy us drinks. I had maxed out every credit card I had—those 18 percent interest cards with $2,000 limits—trying so hard to look like and live like the people we wanted to be around. We hung out in the right crowds, but we were completely broke. So I'd go "buy" the right department store clothing on my department store credit card and then panic at the last minute, put on my old clothes for the party, and return it the next day.

For all of those places I went and trends I followed, I could completely change my look because it was never really *mine* in the first place. My buddy above might not have been polished, but she stayed true to herself. When she knew where she was going, she shifted her wardrobe accordingly. For me, I knew exactly what I wanted to advertise, but I had to figure out how to stay true to myself in the process.

TELL US WHO YOU ARE

We're told to dress for the job we want and not for the job we have, and that's more or less true. If clothing is the billboard that announces to the world who we are and where we're going, the first step is to figure those things out. If you're still working on those early chapter topics, take your time with this chapter.

If you know that your goal is to do well in your job, then a professional wardrobe is part of your long-term planning. If you're going to be outside in your free time and your work, then comfortable, durable clothes are more import-ant. Staying true to that life you want to build has to take precedent over any form of short-term emotional deci-sions, including fashion choices. There's a big payoff that comes with keeping your compass in sight, and a world of consequences if you're controlled by knee-jerk decisions.

The goal is to shift the experience that fashion provides from a temporary emotional bump and toward our long-term goals. If you're only getting an "I deserve this" feeling from overspending on clothes and giving up your ability to save for a house, the investment isn't bringing you meaningful returns.

Fashion doesn't have to be about measuring yourself against the trust fund kid who sits next to you or hiding from the world when you're feeling insecure. It is a tool that can accomplish those things, but there's nothing fierce or future-driven about blending in. If you want to be bold and grow into an assertive, confident woman in control of her life, owning your fashion choices is an important factor.

MAKE IT WORK

With all this internal work that you're doing, fashion is your chance to show the world who you are and who you're becoming. You can do this even within the confines of your industry, your budget, and your body shape.

If you have $400 reserved for a fashion update, look into the most versatile pieces that you need in order to maximize those professional, pricier items. If your budget is tight, try a temporary clothing service like Rent the Runway where you get to pick a few new outfits and send them back when you're done. You can divide up your wardrobe for different environments and moods, then build your budget around those priorities. Go to blow-out bars to let someone play with your hair and experiment with new styles. Get into Sephora to have them do a makeover for you and teach you something new for your makeup routine.

Well-fitting clothes are basically nonnegotiable. They make you feel powerful and confident, and everyone with any goal could use that boost. Dressing appropriately for your environment and context is another confidence booster, sending the message that you belong in the space you're creating. Like it or not, people make decisions about us within twelve seconds of seeing us. Clothes and the way we feel in them get to shape that opinion.

No matter what your limitations are, you can put your own touch on just about anything. It can be as simple as a signature necklace that you always wear, or some staple skirts that make everything look good, or a favorite outfit that you turn to when you want to feel great.

Think about how much different your relationship to fashion would be if you were intentional—not just in the style you choose but with your budget, your goals, and your long-term choices. Find people that you want to model after and see how they're being true to themselves in their choices. Look at the issues that are important to you—the environment or fair trade or certain companies you'd like to support, for example—and bring those into your choices.

There's no way to separate fashion out as its own thing, just like we can't think of any of these other categories as standalone issues. Bringing it in as an integrated part of your life changes the relationship and brings purpose. You're a whole person with your own personality, passion, and purpose, and I can't wait for the world to see you as you are!

PAUSE AND PRACTICE

This exercise is going to take some time. Stick with me, because it's a good one, with two parts. For the first one, you're going to make a fashion-focused vision board. Start with a picture of yourself five years ago and a picture of yourself today. Then add some inspiration pieces from articles, some celebrities or role models (bonus points if they share your Silhouette!), and reminders of your passion focus and the future you're trying to build. This is your compass as you choose your wardrobe and style pieces.

Now, it's time to reach out to your people. Invite someone over—SEAL Team level—who has a good fashion sense and will be honest with you. Let them go through your closet to help you see what doesn't align with your vision, what doesn't look great, and what doesn't represent who you are to the world. Then, it's time to party. Break out the wine and the bags of clothes that you and your friends are decluttering and see what you can trade for. Make sure your vision boards are on full display, so you can keep each other accountable to your goals. Snap a pic of your board or your party and share it with #myshefactor.

CHAPTER ELEVEN

FUEL

FOOD AND FITNESS ARE NOT THE ENEMY

Be stronger than your excuses.

—UNKNOWN

Finally. We're getting into the topics everyone wants to talk about—food, fitness, and in the next chapter, future decisions that are always on our minds. We're always being told how to do more with less and do it better. And that's exactly why we're tackling them last. You can't fix this part of your life until you understand all of the other elements we've been working on. You have to be more confident and brave in seeing how far you can go. You have to be ready to set goals and hold yourself to them.

If you're trying the same things over and over again—losing weight, eating differently, exercising more—and they are not working, it's the definition of insanity. We're here to break those old expectations and patterns in order to create more effective, well-rounded lives.

And honestly? We don't need these concerns to be any bigger than they already are. I'd rather see you thinking more about Faith and Freedom and Folk, for example, than give you another reason to worry about what goes in your mouth. A healthy relationship with Fuel can almost become a by-product of a healthier all-around life.

That's certainly how it worked for me. I promised that I'd tell the full story about Steve, the guy who married someone else while we were dating, and here it is.

COMFORTABLE IN YOUR OWN SKIN

I thought Steve and I had a great relationship, but looking back, I knew deep down we weren't completely on the same page. Even before it ended so strangely, we were just focused on different times in our lives. He was three years older than I was and had already launched his career, and I was still a college kid partying and trying to figure out who I was in the world.

He was also very much into fitness, and I was very much into...having fun.

I was meeting a lot of people and having a great time, while he was really into the relationship and gave up a lot to move to Dallas and then California with me. When he took off traveling with the military, he started to take better care of himself, while I was partying and enjoying my last years in school even more at CU Boulder.

I clearly took our relationship for granted, because I didn't see any reason that we weren't going to get married after graduation. He and I were both back home for Christmas that year, spent a couple weeks enjoying our time together, then went back to our respective lives on a good note. A few weeks later, I got a call from my parents. They'd run into Steve's parents, who awkwardly broke the news. Steve had gotten married the weekend before to a girl he'd met in the Army just a few months before that.

Yes, that's right. I found out third-hand from my parents that my boyfriend of over three years was married to someone else. *Not even a phone call or a letter.* (And we didn't have text or email back then.)

Of course, that set in motion BIG trust issues, but also the opportunity for me to meet and marry Bion in a few years, and the life that brought wonderful and difficult things my way. In that moment, though, I was so angry that he could treat me that way and, maybe more so, that I hadn't seen it coming.

There were some red flags. The first one, of course, was that we didn't have the same priorities. In chapter 5, we talked about the importance of your Flame being a bright spot in your life (and more about this breakup). But also, he was pretty critical about those differences.

When I lost my scholarship to SMU, I decided to move to California to live with my grandparents—pre-low-budget La Jolla—who were from Arkansas and loved to cook "southern comfort" style. Between the partying that I'd done my freshman year and my grandmother's fried chicken I was enjoying, I gained ten or fifteen pounds. And he started to harp on me about it.

He decided to harp on me about it in front of my grand-mother, who adored me as the first girl after her four sons. But he only did it once. She lit into him with her fiery southern accent and let him have it.

Unfortunately, I knew that my grandma would love me no matter what and couldn't care less if I was heavy. Her love came without conditions or consequence. Steve's didn't. His opinion triggered something within me. I thought I had to be skinny or he wouldn't put up with me anymore.

Then, when I went to school in Boulder the next year and everyone in my sorority was super skinny, the messages burrowed even further in.

The sorority house I joined as a transfer at CU Boulder was a top house. I didn't feel like I could be cool enough or thin enough, and neither did they. Eating disorders were rampant in the house. Everyone was always dieting, always working out, and oddly, still drinking as well. When he got married suddenly, it all felt confirmed. I knew I was smart and funny and interesting, so if he would leave me and no one was interested in me, it had to be that one last piece: I was not "skinny" enough.

Never mind that I was only 140-ish pounds at five foot six. The messages rang true, and I couldn't shake them. I couldn't compete with the skinny, petite little things on campus (or, apparently, in the Army). This was, of course, all made up in my head.

It wasn't until Bion came into my life—dashing, accepting Bion—that the narrative in my head began to change. Oddly, as soon as I felt comfortable and loved as I was, the weight started to fall off. No amount of dieting or eating problems could affect me the way that enjoying life and feeling loved as I was could.

This wasn't a one-off case either. After Bion died, I spent

ten years dating pretty horrible people who didn't respect me or treat me well. I convinced myself that I wasn't worth any of the good things that Bion had brought into my life. And then Jason showed up.

I was sure that Jason would turn out to be like all the rest. For a while, I looked for reasons to not trust him, for him to prove that he wasn't any different. But he just wouldn't. He kept reassuring me that he loved me and Tori and wanted to commit to a life with me.

As the doubts and fears melted away, so did my unhealthy patterns, and I once again got comfortable in my own skin.

FUEL YOUR PERSONALITY

The only way to change your relationship with food and fitness is to first get clear on your relationship with yourself. If you don't know why you want to be fit, your efforts won't ever be meaningful. It'll just be another thing on the to-do list.

What's the reward here? They say that feeling fit tastes better than any sweet. Is that true enough to you to give up short-term junk for long-term results? My dear friend Deanna and I have always kidded that we are looking for the "fa-la-la" feeling, where you feel great enough to jump on the bed singing *fa-la-la* because you're so happy in your own skin. We're all more responsive to positive reinforcement than negative, so start with a goal, be kind and encouraging with yourself, and see yourself move toward it.

It's also important to bring your Silhouette into this discussion too. Everyone will have their own style of fitness that appeals to them, and you don't have to force yourself into another mold. A Conqueror who is all about getting sh*t done will want to work out differently than a Kumbaya Dreamer who prefers to save the world and relax afterward, or a Director who doesn't want to be told what to do every day.

If you don't want to be boxed in, then give yourself a menu of options to choose from every day. Get an all-class pass so that you can pick the one that feels right at the time. If you're a Guardian who cares deeply about helping other people, find a workout buddy or a young mentee to coach. Fulfill some of your needs based on your Silhouette, and then food and fitness will begin to fuel you rather than being a drain.

FUEL YOUR PASSION

If you do know why you're working on your relationship to Fuel, you'll have to be willing to commit to realistic goals that fit your personality and lifestyle. It's so easy to push good food and fitness by the wayside when we're ambitiously working toward other goals. But for all of this work that you're doing to build a life of passion and purpose, skipping out on being healthy can become a problem.

Food and fitness can keep us from getting sick. They give us more energy and keep our mood in a good place. They help us to sleep better and wake up ready for the day. Good food and fitness keeps us looking healthy for all that fashion we've spent time and money on and can keep us engaged in better relationships with people who share our goals. Not to mention it's good for the soul.

As with everything else, small efforts do make a difference. Tony Robbins coaches us to sleep eight hours a night and wake up to a high-protein, high-fat breakfast, and our day will go so much smoother.

To get some perspective on what it looks like to bring a better relationship to food and fitness into the life you're building, map out your "dream" schedule. Remember that you've only got a finite amount of time in the day, so it's probably not realistic to look at each goal separately. Think about your perfect job first. When does your day end? What does your commute home look like? How long does it take to change and get to a place to work out? What time is it when you get home? What else did you want to accomplish in your day?

You can't say that you want to win a bodybuilding contest and move up the ladder three times in your career and have a great relationship with your boyfriend. That's not realistic. Most of us fail when we make the stakes too high. We get too aggressive with our goals and fail to plan out the way to actually get there.

You need time to work, spend time with loved ones, have downtime, eat well, and get good sleep. It's going to take some sacrifice and choices. That's okay. You don't have to do everything at once. You can work toward goals in just a couple of areas, then shift them around. Just be aware that it's always a trade-off and that we need to give each facet of our lives some attention in order to grow into well-rounded people.

Keep your ultimate goals in mind, stay focused on your passion, and as my good friend CeCe says at the end of every conversation we have, make good choices.

FUEL UP WITH YOUR PEOPLE

When you're with people who are aligned with your passion and goals in life, you're going to naturally feel more relaxed and will enjoy life together. Steve and I were on such different paths that we didn't do things together or encourage each other. I didn't have time to work out and I ate terribly, while all he did was work out and eat right.

If you hang out with people who drink every night and go to Taco Bell at three in the morning, you're probably not going to reach your fitness goals.

Today, I don't see quite as much pressure to be skinny as when I was in school. Your generation is so much better about being confident in who you are and enjoying life. But at the same time, we're surrounded by social media influencers. Everyone looks amazing on social media, usually because they've been changed in filters and angles and taking forty-five pictures until they look just right.

In theory, the majority of us buy into the desire to be fit and toned and for our skin to glow (as defined by media and influencers), but we've all got so much going on. Fitness almost feels like more work than it's worth. And it is hard work.

It takes constant attention and energy to prioritize good food and fitness. You're never done. Sometimes you have to be committed enough to bravely turn down things that friends and flames want to do that will knock you off of your goals. And on top of it all, the benefits won't be immediate. We don't do well with things that don't offer immediate benefits in today's world, so we get on FaceTune and fake it.

It's hard, but don't give up. You can't just quit food. It's always going to be part of your life. Little by little, one choice at a time, start to build a better relationship with your body and the fuel it needs. We're cheering you on as you do.

PAUSE AND PRACTICE

Small wins are big victories, especially when it comes to food and fitness. For this exercise, spend some time imagining yourself in a better relationship with food. When you think about something, it consumes you, so we're going to think about the wins. Every time you make a choice you can celebrate, write it down. If you chose water, slept eight hours, said no to a drink, fit into a pair of pants, ate a salad, or decided to walk the dog an extra time around the block—those are wins! For bonus points, note whenever a friend helped you feel supported or encouraged you to have a better relationship with food. Shout out some of your wins with #myshefactor.

CHAPTER TWELVE

FUTURE

TRUE SUCCESS IS SUSTAINING A LIFE THAT YOU LOVE

If there's one thing I'm willing to bet on, it's myself.

—BEYONCÉ

Right in the middle of writing this book, I had a birthday. And on that birthday, I found myself on a plane. It made no sense at all to go on the last-minute trip.

I'm busy these days, even though I don't have a paying "job." My plate is very full as I'm on various nonprofit boards, a mom of four, and a CU regent. We work many hours a week just for that role alone, and we don't get paid. To make up for it, we do get some great perks, like all-access parking for all four campuses (which might as well be a pass made of gold). But we also get one really special perk—an away football game that we get to travel to on the team plane, then ride in the police-escort convoy to the stadium and watch from the sidelines in the middle of the action. It just so happened that an away game with our biggest rivals happened on my most recent birthday.

That rivalry goes all the way back to my very first football game at CU. I'd just transferred there, and I felt completely out of place as a new Buff. We definitely shouldn't have won that game; the Buffs' football team was as out of their league as I was that game. But there we were, all out of place together, and CU beat Nebraska, 20–10.

My blood was now black and gold. I was hooked.

And now, it was all coming back full circle. We hadn't played Nebraska since 2010 because of the division changes, but they wanted to reignite the old rivalry with one game this year and another next year. And this one happened on my birthday. On the flight home, we were giddy and exhausted, reeling from a nail-biter win. The team burst out singing the fight song as the plane landed back in Colorado.

It was one of the highlights of my entire career, and I almost didn't go.

Recently, I've been working on making decisions for myself and not for everyone else. When I say no, I try not to explain myself anymore. When I decide what's going to make me happy, I try to push away the urge I have to justify it. It's a skill I've been learning since Camp Bow Wow, when everyone was telling me no and I stepped into my power to do it anyway. I did feel a bit guilty leaving for this trip, though. My nine-year-old, Hollie, and I were just getting past a bout with pneumonia, school had just started, and birthdays are usually a family event. I slipped in the door that Saturday night, thinking at least I'd be home to greet the kids the next morning, and went to sleep so glad that I made the decision to go.

Incidentally, no one even said a word about my birthday until almost noon the next day. They all seemed halfway present (and without any *actual* presents). I'd been so worried about keeping everybody else happy that I almost missed the one thing that I wanted to do.

Now, my family is wonderful, and of course, they made up for it, but this is the lesson I want you to learn, light-years before it ever sank in for me: don't get so caught up in making everybody else happy that you miss out on the future you want to make happen. The one that's right for you.

My life today is wildly different than anything I could

have planned for, and I love every minute. I have a family I love, built a business I'm proud of, and now, spend my time making a difference.

After I sold the company, I was told I should just relax and take it easy. But I had a job to do. I was blessed to live the American dream, and I felt compelled to pay it forward and protect that dream for the next generation. I wanted my children, all children, to live in a land of opportunity so they too could build a business, do what they love, and live the life they imagine. I felt it slipping away with the state of politics, culture, and government policy and wanted to use my time and talents to fight to keep it alive.

I believe education is one key to keeping the American dream alive. But I turned down requests to run for regent three different times before I finally decided to do it. I wasn't convinced running for office was the right way to make a difference. They say that women have to be convinced to run for political office, and I certainly was an example of that.

It was intense. Campaigning for a year was one of the hardest years of my life. My kids often went with me and loved hamming it up on stage, and I worked my butt off. I wanted to show people that we could win with a positive campaign. I wanted to be the change I wanted to see in our party, and in politics in general. And we did it. Our hard work and happy warrior attitude won the day.

FUTURE CAREER

One of the most dangerous things I see young women do is take jobs that are just "fillers" on their resume. Those early job choices do affect your future career. Don't waste your time just getting a job for the sake of a paycheck. Those first opportunities and internships can define you and, if you're not careful, they can box you in. If you're trying to get into advertising, being a receptionist in an ad agency will be a far better choice than a job at a dental office that pays a bit more or carries a bit more responsibility. Once you've chosen a path and know what you're driving toward, it's time to go all in. Do whatever it takes to get your foot in the door. Intern, volunteer, reach out to people that work for the company you want to work for; do whatever it takes to aim for your dream job.

Sometimes, we go all in and then realize it's the wrong direction. As with each of the other categories, we're hiring slow and firing fast. Take your time to decide the path you want to follow, and if you realize it's not actually where you want to be, get out. Make a better decision the second time around, and shift into the career that you want to follow.

You've probably thought about your career—what you want to be when you grow up—since you were little. But we're talking about it last because it's only a piece of your future. It's important to bring everything else that we're working on into your career choice. Your personality, your passions, and the people you'll be around have to be a part of the equation.

Even within your chosen career path, do the work to pick the right company. Check in with yourself—does the company align with who you are and what's important to you? If you know you want to travel a lot, will there be a flexible schedule? If you're planning to have a family, what are their maternity policies like? Interview *them*. Research them. Talk to the people who work there and make sure they have the right attitude and environment so that you can be successful in that environment. You can do a lot of this work before you apply. Just don't be surprised when they are who they say they are. If you find out that they don't give any time off for having a kid, then take the job anyway, don't be surprised if it's a challenge. Be conscientious in each of your decisions.

The choices that you make right now, early on in life, even if you don't feel like you've started your career yet, have an exponential impact on your path in life. As you read this book ready to launch your life, your decisions will be more impactful long-term than the decisions I make in my life as an entrepreneur, author, and elected official in my fifties.

Be intentional about where you apply for jobs, where you're going to live, and who your SEAL Team is, because the jobs you take, the people you surround yourself with, and the way you present yourself will put you into a box and direct your future. It's never too late to get out of that box or change that path, of course, but it's much harder later in life than it is for you now.

FUTURE FAMILY

I hope by now you've caught on—I don't think any aspect of our lives can be checked off like a to-do list, not the least of which is family. Still, we often think that's the case. That having a family is another step toward a successful life, like a foregone conclusion.

If and when you do choose to start a family, you should know that everything is going to change. All your priorities will get shaken up, no matter how hard you try to keep them in a certain order. Your heart lives outside of your chest when you have little ones.

Kids become your top priority, above everything else—career, husband, even self. You'd do anything for them. As much as you can, prepare yourself for that reality.

When you're in a meeting and the school calls to say your kid is sick and you don't have a back-up, guess what? Your child will absolutely come first. We're sold this bill that says we can have it all, but we've already seen that's not true. Every single thing we choose is a choice to take time from something else. And that's the clearest and strongest when your kids are involved.

If you're hoping to have kids in your future, start planning for that now. Make sure your SEAL Team is in place and can help support you through the transition into parenthood. Look at careers and companies that will honor your priorities and won't shut you out of opportunities. Get creative and craft a life around reasonable career and parenting goals. Don't make promises to yourself or your company that things will stay the same, though, because they can't. And that's okay. If that's the decision you want to make, make it with confidence and from a place of empowerment—you're creating your own brilliant future. Don't let anyone hold you back!

With that said, don't forget to choose well when it comes to the person you build a family with, too. It sounds romantic and idealistic to start a family, but I spent the worst five years of my life battling to protect my daughter from someone with a terrible addiction and his enabling mom. I fought like crazy to keep Tori safe. Handing your two-year-old over to someone who you know could very well drink and drive with her or take her to dangerous places in the throes of his addiction is a feeling of fear and desperation that I've never felt since then.

I'd explained it all away to myself before Tori was born. How I knew him so well and could try to make it work. But the decisions we make in the heat of the moment—those short-term, emotion-based decisions—never really take the whole picture into account. "I'm sure we'll be fine" doesn't always play out that way.

There's a concept called the millennial success sequence, which says that taking big milestones in life in a certain order makes your chances of success go through the roof. If you can get at least a high school degree, then a full-time job, then married before having kids, the odds of getting out of poverty or staying out of it are substantial—70 to 90-plus percent.[6] Timing and the right partner are everything, and it's worth waiting and planning for.

Having a baby is going to change your earning power, your career, and your relationship, without question. Whether it's fair or not at this point in our culture, a family becomes its own sphere that requires attention and pulls from the other areas of your life. So don't take chances,

6   W. Bradford Wilcox and Wendy Wang. "The Millennial Success Sequence: Marriage, Kids, and the 'Success Sequence' Among Young Adults." Retrieved on 12/28/2018: http://www.aei.org/publication/millennials-and-the-success-sequence-how-do-education-work-and-marriage-affect-poverty-and-financial-success-among-millennials/.

and don't take this part of your future lightly. Take your time. Be smart about family planning and give yourself the ability to make a clear-headed decision when you're ready and prepared.

FUTURE FOCUSED

Think about where you were when you first started reading this book and where you are now. Has anything shifted? Do you know more about yourself and how you roll? Hopefully, bringing some awareness into your life has changed the way you're looking at your future—from something static and predefined to something dynamic, exciting, and that you can design. The way success looks for you now might not be exactly the same as it was before, or maybe it's similar, but you have a clearer picture of how to get there.

Life for me is so much bigger and bolder and more rewarding than I ever thought it could be. If I hadn't lost Bion, we would have been very happy. I likely would have stayed in pharmaceutical sales, maybe tried to start a little business here or there, and we'd have hopefully had a family that we loved.

But life doesn't usually work that way, even if most of us believe it does when we are starting out.

When I look back on my life, I see so many of those moments where things took an unexpected turn. There was the time I almost lost Camp Bow Wow in the recession, when I fought to protect Tori, when I did lose Bion, when Steve went off and got married, when I unexpectedly met Jason, all the way back to when my parents moved me to Monument from California.

Every step of the way, I got closer to a more powerful, confident version of myself, even if it was brutal sometimes. I'm brave. I'm driven. I don't live by fear anymore. I'm bold and I'm feisty and I live the changes that I want to see.

That's because this topic of your *future* is not one that you can always control. Your parents, your teachers, and your boss can't decide what it looks like. It's more of a culmination of this full life that you're building—it's allowing yourself to dream those big crazy dreams, then letting life take you into places you couldn't have imagined. As long as you keep coming back to that compass of who you are and what you want out of life, your future will be bright, bold, and amazing, just like you.

PAUSE AND PRACTICE

For this last exercise, take a few hours with a bunch of magazines and printouts and a glass of wine. It's time to make another vision board, but this time we're digging into all of it together. Let yourself dream about the future you're driving toward. How do you dress? How do you spend your time? Who are you with? Where do you live? What do you know about yourself now, and what do you hope to learn as you grow? This is the last step for this book, but the first one for you. Now it's time to hold yourself accountable and make your dreams come true. Snap a pic of your completed board and share it at #myshefactor.

CONCLUSION

Taking the next step after graduation is hard. You have had 16+ years in a programmed environment. You are now truly on your own with many decisions to make—new job, new friends and perhaps a new place to live. Be bold, strike out to drink it all in and take risks. Do not be afraid.

—DONNA LYNNE, CHIEF EXECUTIVE OFFICER,
COLUMBIA DOCTORS; CHIEF OPERATING OFFICER,
COLUMBIA UNIVERSITY MEDICAL CENTER;
LT. GOVERNOR OF COLORADO 2016–18

There's no better educator in life than experience. When we can share in the experiences of other people through their stories and learned wisdom, it's almost as good. It warms my heart to have had the opportunity to share my experiences with you. I hope that you've connected to some of the words in this book, or that you've seen parts of yourself in the things that I've tried and failed and won and lost. I hope that the path in front of you is a little clearer because of our time together on these pages.

When Tori was graduating college and starting off in the world, I wanted to give her something like this book. Then as I started to write it, I realized that the twenty-year-old me needed it just as much.

I know what you're up against, and I know the world today is that much more difficult to navigate than the one I grew up in. Your world is changing every single day.

But what the world doesn't know is just how much you're growing too. You're part of an incredibly bright and caring generation who wants to make the world a better place. You should be celebrated.

You shouldn't be punished for wanting work-life balance or choosing to not have a family or choosing to stay home with your kids. You shouldn't be punished for wanting parental leave or to work from home with your dog. You should be supported at every turn—by *yourself*—because it's up to you.

I grew up surrounded by amazing women. My aunts were incredibly strong. My grandmas and my mom were amazing. My mom's best friends were wonderful to me. I was the first grandchild and the first girl after so many boys. (I got so much attention!) That tribe of women shaped who I believed I could be, and my uncles and dad and grandfather supported me in it.

If you don't have that kind of support, find it. If you can't find it in your family, your flame, or your current group of friends or coworkers, the SheFactor women are here for you, to fill in the gaps where others can't. Take the time to download the app so you can track each of these Spheres in your own life. Connect with your nearest meetup group. Find a SheFactor champion and build your SEAL Team. Start there, because this is just the start of your journey. You have an adventure ahead of you. You're going to want to build the best support system you can.

We're a community—not only SheFactor, but all of us together. That's what we need more of in society—people who are willing to honor each other and build each other up as we work together to create a new future. That's having a present power. That's building a future fierce.

That's our SheFactor.

ACKNOWLEDGMENTS

I'm eternally grateful to my beautiful daughter, Tori, for bringing me back from heartbreak when she came into my life twenty-plus years ago. Thank you for taking me on a wonderful journey as your mom, filled with joy, love, laughter, and lots of worry, of course. I'm so proud and happy to share your stories alongside my own in the advice shared in this book.

To my family. Mom and Dad, thank you for your constant love and support, and your consistent belief that I can do anything I set my mind to! Thank you for instilling in me the value of hard work and the importance of keeping my word. Patrick, thank you for your belief in me back when I didn't even believe in myself. Jason, thank you for your love and support as I've created *SheFactor*, and tolerating my constant interruptions for your opinions from the couch. Hollie, Jack, and Jenna, I love you with all my heart, and you inspire me to make the world a better place every day!

To my amazing aunts. Debbie, Cathy Jo, Jean, Lisa, Colleen and Marsha, Diane and Kerry, you gave me all the love, confidence, and strength I needed to believe I could go out and conquer the world. Thank you so much. I love you all.

To my friends. You are my rocks and inspire me every day. You've been on this journey with me and filled it with love, care, and compassion. You are amazing!

To Don, Whitney, and Keith. You taught me so much and were there for me in so many ways. I'm most grateful for the permission you gave me to be myself and lead my own way.

To my team at Scribe—Brannan, Kayla, and Erin—what a wonderful experience you made this. Thank you from the bottom of my heart!

To all my furry friends who helped me live my best life caring for you and building the business of my dreams, woof!

And to Bion, Ma and Da, Mum and DaHenry, David and Jackie—you are in these pages and in my heart forever.

Bion and Heidi on their honeymoon, Southern California, 1992

Kirk, Heidi, and Tori at Tori's kindergarten graduation

Heidi and Jason's wedding at The Palazzo, 2009

Heidi and her beloved grandma, Ma, 2012

Double trouble, 2012

Heidi's brother, Patrick, hosting Camp Bow Wow's Music for Mutts fundraiser.

Heidi and a happy camper at Camp Bow Wow

Photoshoot for *Fortune* magazine, 2015—"Finding Her Wow in Camp Bow Wow"

Wall Street Journal article, the day Camp Bow Wow sold, 2014

Tori and Ray Ray, Heidi's partners in building Camp Bow Wow

Tori's graduation from the University of Oregon, 2017

Mom, Dad, Patrick, Ma, and Heidi, back to our Arkansas roots for a family reunion

Heidi and her partner in crime, Deanna, Broncos game, 2018

Best friends from the start, Heidi and Dawn Marie

Campaigning with my team—Jill, Monica, and Andie—2016

"The Art of the Comeback" at TEDxMileHigh, 2015

Speaking at the Young Women's Leadership Summit, 2016

Heidi on Folsom Field, CU Boulder, on the campaign trail

Family photo, 2018